MW00949563

Heaven Is
A
Real Place

GAYNOR CARRILLO

Also By Gaynor Carrillo

Always By Your Side: True Life Stories From The Life Of
A Psychic Medium

DEDICATION

I dedicate this book to my beloved Nana Wasdell, who left my life before the final chapter.

Acknowledgements
I could not have written this book if it wasn't for the continual support of my family.

My husband who has lost me for hours while I have typed away.

My son Danny, who has spent endless hours helping me with all kinds of background issues on this book and for all the laughter along the journey.

My daughter Nicole, for being a constant support for me and always being there for me.

My mother, for being my friend and for keeping me laughing.

You are all the light of my life.

To all the Spirits who have been kind enough to let me into their world and who have entered into mine throughout my lifetime to share messages and insight.

Thank you.

Thank you for all my clients who have come to me for readings over the many years I have been doing this work.
A special thank you to all who have allowed me to use your stories in this book.

CONTENTS

PART FOUR – HAPPY IN HEAVEN

Introduction

Is Heaven a real place? A client asked me recently while I was giving them a reading. I wasn't surprised by the question, as I have had the same question asked to me many times during the two decades I have been working as a psychic medium.

What happens when we die? Is there life after death? Is there really a Heaven? Do we join with our loved ones? Do we reunite with our pets? These are just some of the questions I am asked daily in my work.

Over the years, I have answered by recounting many of the stories that Spirit has told me, and in this book, I now relate them along with snippets from my own wonderful adventures in Heaven, in order to answer those very questions.

As far as I am aware, I have never had a near death experience. There was a time some years ago when I almost died due to loss of blood after a small operation. Unfortunately, there was no near-death story to share on waking.

Luckily, I have never been involved in any type of near-death impact. I have never fallen on my head, fallen down a mountain or been involved in a car crash. Nothing has ever happened to me where I can say that from that moment onwards, I started to visit the Spirit world.

However, my entire life I have been able to enter the Afterlife and explore the world beyond ours. For a long time, I called this magical world "the place," and my visits there have always been random and unexpected.

My adventures were also unpredictable in how long I stayed in "the place." Sometimes I felt as if I had visited for minutes, other times it felt like I had spent the entire day.

I have no real concept of time in the Spirit world. I believe this is because time as we know it does not exist in Heaven. However, I do know I spent a lot of "time" exploring the wonders of the Afterlife.

I was also born with the ability to see Spirits and I have used this gift wisely by working as a medium. I have had the pleasure to give readings for thousands of people from around the world. I wrote about this subject in more detail in my first book, Always by Your Side.

I had an unusual childhood due to seeing Spirit, dreaming vivid dreams every night, entering the Afterlife, and knowing things were going to happen before they did. However, I was not born knowing I wanted to be a medium. Instead, I had a very strange and passionate love for the tarot cards.

From a young age, my dream was always to be a tarot card reader. I was intrigued as a child with the images of the cards and the thought of being able to predict the future was thrilling and exciting for me. I wanted magic powers where I could tell people's futures. I was so used to seeing Spirit that it never bothered me or inspired me in any way. I didn't see anything special or magical about seeing Spirit.

My lack of excitement for seeing Spirit and the Spirit world changed after my dad died when I was thirteen. It was a hard time for me because I felt he left my life before I ever truly received the love and attention I so desperately sought. I was heartbroken and lost in grief. I desperately needed to know where he was. I needed to find him in the Afterlife.

For the first time ever, I realised how important it was to know that a loved one is safe and well after they had died. There was never any doubt in my mind that those who have passed still exist. Yet, I needed to know more on the subject. I started to question the Afterlife in the hope of understanding more about the death of my dad. I questioned and explored my own childhood experiences. I had now commenced my spiritual quest.

It was when I was in my teens and studying tarot cards that I realized I also wanted to become a medium. After all, I had seen Spirit since I was born, and I had communicated with them almost daily.

I soon realized that talking to the dead and becoming a working medium are very different concepts. I worked hard to become a medium, being as honest as I could and accepting my limitations. I made mistakes in my work and there were days I felt I wasn't worthy of such a job.

I talk to Spirit the same way they talk to me, through mind. It's as if my mind becomes my voice box and thought is quicker than speech so I can hear a lot and say a great deal in what seems like seconds.

Understanding the process of working with Spirit was like working inside a huge jigsaw puzzle. Yet I felt without doubt it was my path and I continued to learn and understand as to how to communicate with Spirit to be able to pass on messages to their loved ones.

My spiritual quest brought me to where I am today. A full time working medium and still a tarot card reader, I was never able to water down my passion for tarot cards.

One of the biggest pleasures I have in my work is answering questions my clients ask me about the Afterlife. I love talking about Spirit and the world where they reside.

Describing the Spirit world is often hard because it is so amazingly vibrant, magical, and alive with nature, but also because it is so immense and varied.

If someone was to ask me to describe this earthly world, I may or may not describe to them the freezing cold waters of the Antarctica with its white landscape and icy rocks. I may not mention the blaring heat of the Sahara and its miles of waterless desert. I may briefly mention the huge green rainforest of the Amazon and its importance in our planet.

I will however talk in detail about the wonders of Spain, the hot summer days with the sparkling blue sea and the rough, rugged mountains that lay backdrop to the endless blue sky. I will also talk about the wet green grass of England, the crisp cold air on an early winter morning that leaves the earth a pale shade of white.

The Spirit world is much the same for me, I can describe in detail the areas I know and have visited. I can briefly talk about places I know are there and are of importance, yet I have never had the privilege of exploring.

I use a colourful selection of words to describe the magical Spirit dimension that is just within our reach. The Other side, the Afterlife, the Spirit world, the place, are all words I use to describe what is more commonly known as Heaven and are words repeatedly used by my clients.

As I was writing this book, Spirit inspired me in such a way that was rather incredible. I felt the presence of Spirit within every page, encouraging me to have no fear to share with others my most intimate adventures.

I received emails asking me the exact same question I had just answered in this book. After logging onto my Facebook page, I found an image posted that was almost identical to a scene I had just written. It was as if a painter were standing behind me and painting my very words. While writing each chapter I would suddenly hear its title name said on the TV or from people I met on that same day.

It was thanks to these many signs from Spirit that I was able to write about Heaven even despite my fear of being criticised about such an emotive subject. I now face the wind and share with you, not only many Spirit stories, but also my own true-life accounts of the immense Afterlife.

As you may have gathered by now, I'm not a doctor or a scientist and I have no religious background. So why should I write a book about something as grand as the Afterlife, I mean it doesn't get any bigger than this, we are talking HEAVEN.

The reason is that I do have the answers to many of these important questions that people ask me daily. I know what happens when we die. I know what happens to our loved ones when they pass over, I know how the process works, and most important of all, I know that Heaven is a real place.

PART ONE

ALL KINDS OF WONDERS

CHAPTER 1

Life Before Life

I believe the beginning does not start when we are born into the physical world. Far from it, before we join this earthly world, we are very much alive in the Afterlife. We have a full, happy, content life in a world far better than this one.

We live a very active life in the Spirit world doing activities much as we do in this world, like studying, working, and playing. We enjoy art and music.

We have a huge spiritual family who we have shared many lifetimes with, we have friends, hobbies and we have a home.

At some point, we decide to return to the physical world. This is something that is discussed and planned in great detail. The reason we return to this world, for what can only be described as a holiday, is personal to every one of us. This may explain why the question of "why are we here?" is hard to answer, because we are all here for our very own individual reason.

Our return journey to this earthly world takes a great amount of planning, each aspect of our journey has to concede in helping us reach our life purpose, the "why am I here."

We plan our trip entwined with others who we are close to in the Spirit world, I call these other Spirits our Spirit family. We work very closely with them when we plan our holiday to this world. The return journey takes a lot of intense planning.

Many of our Spirit family will return on this trip with us, not on the same day, some will come earlier, and others will arrive just as we are about to return to the Spirit world after our own earthly existence. The roles of who will play what part is planned out very much like the characters in a book, who will be our father, our mother, our children, and just like a book we discuss in detail what part we will all play in the lives of each other. All based around each one of us reaching our life purpose and hopefully having a good time while here.

This probably isn't the first time we did this, we have planned and ventured many lifetimes together. In one way or another, we have always travelled with the same Spirit family, always taking on a different role, returning in another body, with an entirely different relationship to each other.

Although our life is very well mapped out for this trip back here to the physical world, we know we will have certain points that our free will can control. That's supposed to be the fun part of the trip, enjoying our free will in the hope we make the correct choices in life.

To help us on this exciting trip back to the earthly world, a member of our Spirit family will choose not to return with us this time. Instead, they will decide to stay in the Spirit world and help guide us with our life plan, hoping that we will reach our true potential, live out our life purpose and enjoy the trip. This act of staying behind to guide us each step of the way is one of the kindest acts of love known to Spirit.

When we are planning our physical lifetime, we are fully conscious of all our previous lifetimes and how we have all been connected to each other in each life. We plan a lot of our next journey based on things we learnt in our previous journeys. As if a huge saga had been running throughout each of our lifetimes, and although we return each time as a different character, the background story is all connected. We plan everything for a reason. We are the writers of our own sagas and co-writers with everyone who touches each page.

When we are planning and writing our life stories, we watch as others from our Spirit family temporary leave us to start their own journey. We watch them and it is with excitement and joy we say good-bye to them, knowing we will be seeing them shortly, when we ourselves also make the exit from the Spirit world to the earthly world.

We give them a farewell, as we know they are part of our journey, and we are part of theirs. The next time we will be seeing them will be in a physical form and they will have become our mother, father, friend, or foe, depending on what role we have all chosen.

As we say our goodbye, we continue our life in the Spirit world, and we know that "soon" we will be taking that same journey back to have the "trip of a lifetime."

Suddenly the day is getting nearer. Our stars are aligned for our very own time to live a physical life, our "lifetime."

We feel the love around us from those in our Spirit family who have not yet left, those that will later become our children, our grandchildren, and those who will follow us to meet us in the later years. They are as excited for us as we are for them, and they know that we are about to embark on our journey and at some point, they will join us.

The excitement is seeing if we can reach our true potential. Not only are we excited about the physical aspect of life and all the physical senses, including touch. We are also happy about being part of the physical world. We are eager to be able to swim in the sea and feel the water in the physical sense. We are excited to be able to walk with the wind in our hair, to feel a human touch, not in a Spiritual way but in a living physical way.

Although in the Afterlife we can live each one of these experiences in a much bigger and better way, yet we experience it with our Spirit through the mind. Everything in the Spirit world is created with the mind. Although it outstands any physical experience, we are still excited to return. We look forward to that first touch, being hugged by our mothers or maybe even that first kiss.

The timeless period before we return to our earthly life is a busy period, we constantly check all the last details. Completing any unfinished work we may have in the Spirit world and preparing our goodbyes. At some point, we have a final review. We sit with that Spirit member who is to become our guide and we re-live our yet unlived life step by step.

This is the point we may feel anticipation, we can only hope that we don't fail ourselves and that we are able to live the life we truly wanted to. Our guide has promised to help us along the way, showing us signs and guiding us in any way possible. Will we be strong enough to find the signs and follow the guidance?

We also discuss in detail the hardships that we have included in our journey, those important yet darker times. We wonder if we will fully understand when that time comes that even the harder times are part of our destiny, will we accept it as that? Even though we can see the bigger picture now, we know the story, we co-wrote it. However, will we be able to remember? To trust that even the darker pages of our life are also part of our life story.

The one thing we hope for is to enjoy the journey. Because we know, no matter what, the final destination is to return home to the Spirit world.

We say our goodbyes. It is now time for our earthly holiday. We feel excitement and joy as we take the short walk between worlds.

Suddenly the bright lights of the Afterlife become dimmer and dimmer until we find ourselves surrounded by darkness; we have come from such light that this darkness is somehow pleasant. We float around this dark emptiness, yet we are not floating aimlessly, we know we have somewhere to go.

The Spirit world, the place we have just left and where we have been for the last eternity, now feels somewhat far away, and our mind starts to feel drowsy. We know we are floating in a dark space, yet we begin to feel almost like we are floating in a sea of water, our memories start to fade ever so slowly. We know we have a plan, a life purpose, a destiny, and yet we become sleepier and sleepier within the darkness, until suddenly we forget, and we sleep.

We haven't even realized that we have entered our mother's womb.

CHAPTER 2

Best Of Both Worlds

The screams echoed around the hospital as my mum felt every second of her painful two-day labour. On a cold English winter night, the clocks had just past midnight and January was two days away from ending, I was born.

I don't remember that day or the following days. However, I do remember looking around me while I was lying in my cot not long after being born, and realizing this was it, I was here.

I remember a lot of my life as a child. I wasn't breastfed and I remember the milk my mother gave me had a funny smell, almost repugnant. I clearly didn't like the flannelling nappies that were pinned around me daily, they were stiff and would irritate me. I didn't like the way I was rocked most of the time in the hope I would sleep, and I didn't like everyone picking me up and being passed around. I was mostly happy when I was outside in my pram. In my first pram, I laid on my back and I remember clearly looking above me and seeing the grey English sky following me. I would look at the clouds and go dizzy watching them pass me by.

Then I grew old enough to have a sit-down pram. I was now able to turn my head freely and have a better view when outside, enabling me to see more than just the grey sky.

I didn't like being indoors and all indoor memories I had were dark until I was around the age of one and my dad and one of his close friends painted a huge mural on the wall for me. Looking back, I find it ironic that they had painted a scene from Alice in wonderland. They had no idea I was living in my own wonderland.

My Play Land

From as young as my memory started to record, I remember clearly going back to the Afterlife. I didn't know it as anything other than "the place" and this continued for many years. I would freely go to this amazing place in my dreams, sometimes I didn't want to return to this world, preferring the magical place of my dreams. This would often cause me to wake up screaming.

My mum remembers with shudders how I cried almost day and

night for the first year of my life. She could do nothing to stop me from crying. Yet I remember my cries were not because I was unhappy. I was just expressing myself in the only way I knew how. I would rather laugh if I was happy or I would scream if I was uncomfortable, mostly I was uncomfortable.

I do remember very clearly the journeys in my dreams of the magical place I felt I had once called home. Over time, I slowly started to forget who I really was during these journeys. I'm not sure when it happened, but at some point, in my early childhood, while I was in the magical wonderland of my dreams, I no longer remembered my life before life. Although vague memories would come and go, instead I became Gaynor. I would visit as who I was, a little girl.

From then onwards, I would dream I was in the place, and I had no memory of who I had been before, where I was going, or why. Instead, I had exciting new experiences. I played freely when I was in the "the place". I met friends when there and I laughed, danced, and enjoyed each visit to the enchanted land. I spent a great deal of my childhood back and forth between another world and this world through the doorway of my dreams.

In Between Worlds

In this world, I lived between my Nana's house and my mums, mainly due to my mums work. The alternative would be that my mum would have to wake me up early on cold English winter mornings and drop me off at my Nana's on her way to work. My mum and my dad had separated when I was only one year old, it was, therefore, easier for me if I stayed at my Nana's.

I loved living with both. When I lived with my mum, we would often pass many hours watching old films together and she would spoil me rotten. I would have the best clothes and she would take me to the finest restaurants. We would play together for hours, and she always expressed her love for me. My mum was young and full of fun. She had an "I don't care" attitude about her, and she certainly didn't care about the same things Nana did. She didn't count every penny or worry about tomorrow's dinner. Instead, she was spontaneous, adventurous, and very kind-hearted. It was thanks to my mum's adventurous soul that I had a happy upbringing along with adventures other children my age did not have. I have lived in some interesting places and met a variety of exciting people thanks to my mum's constant travels. Even today, we look back at our adventures and laugh together as we remember.

A Not So Normal Life

When I lived at my Nana's house, I would take walks in the park with my Granddad or help him with the big fruit and veg plot he had created in his back garden. I would bake cakes with my Nana, who loved me immensely. Throughout my life, I always felt my Nana and Granddads home was my home. I felt much loved there.

The house itself was full of Spirit activity. I would often walk into a room and randomly see a Spirit person just appear and disappear before my eyes. I think when something happens since birth it isn't really questioned, and I don't ever remember questioning why I was seeing Spirit. I was never scared nor excited at seeing

Spirits. It seemed to have had no effect on me as a child at all.

I was never scared of the Spirits I saw at my Nana's house, instead I was more worried about having to run up to the toilet in the evening due to the freezing cold house that became a huge ice box once I opened the living room door. I would run up the stairs to the toilet only after I knew I could not hold myself any longer. The warm heat of the living room would stay inside the living room, as the icy cold temperatures of the house would make me shiver. Often, I would run to the toilet and as I left, I would see a Spirit on the landing. Shivering with cold, I would ignore the Spirit and run downstairs to the heat of the living room, without giving much thought to the Spirit I had just seen.

Micheal

It was when I was very young that I realised one same Spirit man was always around me and he did affect me in many ways. I would talk to him and listen to him. The Spirit was a slim man with beautiful, peaceful eyes and a slim face. When I wasn't seeing him as Spirit, I could hear his voice in my head or feel his presence and sense him. For years, I knew him as the voice in my head. Now I know him as Micheal, (and yes spelt that way). He is my guide and my friend.

Micheal is the one I have always turned to for advice when I have had any kind of problem or dilemma throughout my life. Not only in my day-to-day life, but also in my work as a psychic medium. Not that he replies as one would expect an evolved guide to reply. No, instead, I somehow find the answer after he has guided me to it.

Unexpected Meditation

I was no longer an infant when purely by accident I realized I could also reach my play land through a type of meditation. While wide-awake, I was able to switch my mind off from whatever was happening around me and I was able to allow my physical body to be still while my mind began to explore and play in the Other world. At the time, I didn't know I was meditating. It was just something that happened to me naturally.

I really hated school. I found it pointless and boring until one day in class, my teacher was talking, and his words started to fade into the background. At that point, I was no longer listening to my teacher. Instead, I was listening to the sound of water.

My eyes were wide open yet inside my mind, I was no longer in the classroom. I had found my way to escape class and I found myself standing beside a flowing river. I could hear birds in the trees that surrounded me. I looked up at a huge tree. I knew I was in the place of my dreams because the tree was alive with energy. The water was almost musical, and the air was crystal clear, almost as if there was no air.

I noticed a bench overlooking the river. I sat on the bench and felt complete bliss with the nature that surrounded me. The musical notes of the flowing water had an almost hypnotic effect on me. I was amazed I was in "the place" yet I was wide-awake.

I was abruptly brought back to my surroundings and children were now standing up around me and chairs were being dragged around the classroom floor.

The entire episode had opened a doorway for me and from that moment onwards, I was able to reach my dreamland by this form of unplanned meditation.

CHAPTER 3

I Dreamed a Dream

At some point in my early childhood I realised that this Other world was the Spirit world, the Afterlife. I'm not sure when I figured it out, but I feel somehow, I had always known. It was just not something I questioned with importance.

When I wasn't in the Spirit world in my dreams, then I was there due to meditation. It was when I was around ten years old that another change occurred within me, or should I say around me.

At this time, I had been living in a small flat in London with my mum, her then husband Mehmet and my stepsister Yeshim, who was from Cyprus. Yeshim was a few years younger than I was. Because I was an only child, I enjoyed suddenly having a stepsister. Yeshim spoke very little English, and I taught her quickly how to speak my language. We were very close, and I love her dearly.

Jumping Into Heaven

This one cold day I had walked Yeshim to her school then I headed in the direction towards my own school. It had been miserably drizzling with rain most of the morning, but it had now started to rain heavily and within minutes, the rain was pelting down hard. I started to run to school. Rain was dripping off my nose and my hair was drenched so I picked up my speed and ran as quick as I could towards my school.

As I ran at an almost sprinting speed and quicker than I can ever remember doing so, I noticed the rain was no longer falling on me. In fact, as I ran, I noticed the sun was now shining bright. I stopped dead in my tracks and as I looked around me, I saw I was in the midst of the countryside. I could see miles of green fields and as I looked above me and saw the baby blue sky, I knew exactly where I was, but how?

I continued to walk forward slowly. I could smell the green grass of the countryside. I could hear nature gently growing around my feet. I was mesmerised with the miles of greenery that surrounded me. I realised I was completely alone and yet the familiar sounds of nature brought a smile to my face. I felt immersed in love, as if the sun was warming me with rays of pure love.

I noticed hundreds of dandelions by my feet, and I bent down and picked one, gently breaking its dark green stem. I loved blowing dandelions and playing silly question and answer games or the clock game. As I knelt down on the grass, I smiled as I blew. The tiny white umbrella like seeds flew around me. What should have been a handful of almost whisper like fluffy seeds, turned into hundreds of them. As the umbrella seeds scattered all around me, almost dancing in the air, I stared with excitement as I saw how each seed landed on the ground and immediately the dance of nature and regrowth began to happen before my eyes.

At that moment, everything around me turned shades darker. I found myself still running at a sprinting speed and rain was dripping down my nose. Again, I stopped and stood still. This time, the toxic smell of car fumes invaded my nose and the hustle and bustle of London surrounded me.

I was completely intrigued as to how I had suddenly been transported to the Other World.

A few nights later, I dreamt I was in the Spirit world with George, one of the older boys who was around 17 years old. George lived in the Spirit world, and I had known him all my life when visiting. He watched over my Spirit friends and me. George was like a big brother to us all and he would often take us exploring the Afterlife. This particular visit, I told George about what had happened to me. "I was just running really fast, then I was here in this world, and I was wide awake," I said to him rather surprised at my own adventure.

"You better get used to it," he said to me. "When it happens once it's going start happening regularly," he added with a rather cheeky grin on his face. I wondered to myself what he meant when he said "it" happens.

The London Bus

Over the next few years, "it" did start happening to me a lot. I would find myself here in this world and randomly my surroundings would change, and I would find myself in the Afterlife. This would happen to me while I was at the park, walking in the street, in a playground, lying in bed, almost anywhere.

Once it happened to me when I was on a bus in London. I had been sitting on the bus and I knew my stop was the next stop. Suddenly, as I looked through the dirty windows, I found myself sitting on very long grass. Amazed at my change of surroundings, I stood up and walked around, almost jumping over the long grass. I saw a pathway in the distance, and I headed towards it and decided to take a walk and see where it led me.

I noticed a couple walking towards me. They appeared almost transparent and were transmitting a huge amount of colourful energy that was twirling from within them, yet I could see clearly what they looked like. I was used to seeing Spirit with such immense colours surrounding them and shining from them. As they passed me, they both smiled. I could see they were happy, and I smiled back. "Should you be here?" the man stopped and asked me.

"I don't know," I replied rather awkwardly. He smiled at me, and I continued to walk onwards. I saw a field that looked familiar, and I noticed a house with a large barn outside. Immediately I knew where I was. I had been here before with some friends in several dreams. I remembered we had played with the animals in the field. I ran over to the field and there I saw the animals. I sat and played with them for what seemed like hours.

A bumblebee was flying around me the entire time. I wasn't scared of being stung because I knew it wouldn't sting me.

Taking a break from playing, I lay back on the grass. I could easily lie here forever, I thought to myself. As my head touched the soft blades of grass, immediately I was transported back to the dirty windows of the old London bus.

As these transportation's were random, I could never predict when they would happen. Nor could I control my meditations. I also didn't know what nights I was going to enter the Afterlife in my dreams or not. Every day and night was an adventure for me as I could very well spend it in this world or the other.

I loved the Spirit world. However, I also loved the physical world. I enjoyed every moment I was here just as I did when I was "there."

In the living world, I would play with my cousin Amanda, who was almost like a sister to me. I would go shopping for hours with my Nana, helping her hunt out the bargains in endless selections of shops. I would sit for hours with my Granddad and play games like chess and snakes and ladders. My entire life was a good fun place to be. Although I was different to others that I knew. I had the best of both worlds. I could see random Spirits and I also had Micheal, the voice in my head, who talked to me daily about anything and everything.

I could also see auras. Glows of different colours surrounding people's bodies. Although the colours were a much flatter and a paler version of what I saw surrounding Spirits in the Afterlife. I thought everyone could see these colours on people until I realized when I was older that not everyone could see these auras.

I also knew things before they would happen. It was often not things of importance, but I knew many things before they happened. Friends and family would tell me things, or something would happen, and I used to be confused and think to myself, I know all this, I knew all this was going to happen.

I was having a strange existence and I never told anyone. As if traveling to the Afterlife or seeing Spirits wasn't strange enough for a child, I had other unusual and strange happenings constantly happening around me.

My Friend at the Bottom of the Garden

I had just returned from a holiday with my mum from Ibiza in Spain. I learnt how to swim and had a fantastic time. On my return home, I dreamed I was in the Afterlife, playing with my friends. I noticed George was talking to a young girl around my age. I walked over to them, and we began to play. I told her all about my holiday to Ibiza and I excitedly told her how I had learnt to swim. "I can swim too," she said to me, nodding her head with enthusiasm. We both turned and looked at George and asked him if we could go for a swim. He agreed and he took us to a short cut to a lake.

For a long time, my friend and I played and swam together in the waters of the Afterlife, with not one care in the world. I opened my eyes underwater and swam like a fish.

A few days after my dream, my mum and I went to my Nana's house for a visit. I told my Nana all about my adventure of Ibiza then I went into the back garden to play.

My Nana's back garden was a world of its own. My Granddad had created two big fruit and vegetable plots out the back where he would grow all kinds of treasures for my Nana to cook. At the bottom of the garden was huge hedges. These hedges separated us from another garden that belonged to someone else, the neighbour behind us. There was always a small opening within the hedges, and I could see the other garden clearly. Although a thin wire fence and huge bushes made it unreachable. I noticed some children were playing in the garden and I peeked through the bushes to have a look, then I saw my friend who I had been swimming with in my dreams a few days before.

"Hiya," she said, recognizing me immediately. We continued our friendship as we had in the Spirit world. We talked about our swimming adventure and even talked about how clever George was finding us a shortcut to the lake.

However, playing through a small gap in the fence was boring. My mum came out and asked me who I was talking to. I told her she was my new friend, and I begged my mum to let me walk all around the block to go and play in my friends back garden.

My mum was having none of it, my pleas fell onto empty ears. "Too far," she claimed, dismissing the idea. "But it's only at the bottom of the garden," I pleaded as I tried convincing her, but I knew it wasn't just at the bottom of the garden. I would have to walk all the way around the block to her house to get into her garden and I knew my mum wouldn't let me go to a stranger's house.

"Where do you know her from?" my mum asked suspiciously when I accidentally mentioned we had been swimming together.

"From Ibiza," I lied. "Yes, we went swimming in Ibiza," my friend said, popping her face against the small opening.

Big mistake, my mum thought it would be great to talk to my friend's parents and ask where in Ibiza they had stayed. Insisting on speaking to the girl's parents through the gap in the fence, my mum asked questions. That is when she was told that my friend had not been abroad recently. We must have been mistaken.

I don't know why I didn't tell the truth, that I had met my friend in a dream and that we had gone swimming for the day. The fact that my friend remembered clearly playing with me and she remembered the entire day as I did should have been proof enough. Plus, she told me she went there all the time and George knew her. However, I didn't tell my mum the truth. Instead, the Ibiza story hadn't worked and now I definitely wasn't allowed to go and play with her.

In this world, I never saw that girl again. Apparently, she was only in the house behind my Nana's visiting the owners with her parents for that day. Yet in my dreams, I saw her on several occasions. We picked up our friendship just as we left it each time and over the years, we witnessed how we both grew into little women.

The Boy at the Lake

Sometime after the incident with the girl at the bottom of the garden. Another incident happened to me one night while I was dreaming I was in the Spirit world. I had been wandering and exploring very much alone. I knew Spirit was around, yet I was busy playing with nature and wasn't really paying attention to what was happening around me.

I was standing by a large lake, and as I looked into the water, I could see thousands of bright multi-coloured fish. I stood in childlike wonder as I observed how the fish swam beneath the clear almost transparent water. I knew there was a game being played between the fishes and I tried to work out what the game was.

"It's like hide and seek." I heard a man's voice say to me. Startled, I turned, and I saw my schoolteacher. Surprised to see him I just smiled at him and continued to watch the fish. I hadn't been at that school for long and I hardly knew this teacher. He had always appeared rather miserable and stern to me and at school, I had never really felt much need to talk to him.

"Where do they hide?" I asked him, wondering where these amazing brightly coloured fishes would hide and wishing I were playing with them.

"Come with me, I will show you." My teacher said as he pulled his knees up to his chest and jumped into the water.

I watched as he went under the clear water, then his head

popped up and he laughed. "Jump in," he indicated to me.

I dived into the water, gliding down, with my eyes open. The sun was reflecting within the water. I came up for air and as I came up, I noticed a small boy had joined my teacher. He was around six years old with white, blond hair.

"Let's go," the teacher said to us both as he bopped down within the water. All three of us swam underwater in the large lake. The boy and I followed the teacher until we came to a huge opening.

As we entered the huge rocky opening under the water, I realized I had not needed to swim to the surface for air. It was an exciting moment when I realized I didn't need air. I quickly compared myself to a mermaid and entered the opening with excitement.

What was on the other side of the opening underneath the lake was spectacular.

The lake, which was now behind us, was a small drop of water compared to the huge clear waters we now found ourselves. The water was almost as clear as the air and I could see for miles around me while under the water. We followed the fish swimming in and out of small rocks and vibrant colourful plants. The teacher pointed between rocks and plants, showing us where the fish were hiding. The fish almost teased us with their games, almost as if they knew we were watching them and enjoying their playtime with them.

Every now and then, we would swim to the surface of the water, not for air but just for fun. From the surface, we could see beaches around us, miles upon miles of golden beaches in the near distance. It appeared we were now somehow in the middle of the ocean. We laughed as we waded through the water.

The little boy lay down on his back and floated, closing his eyes and relaxing. The teacher swam underneath him and then flipped him over. We all laughed, and the boy splashed the teacher vigorously spraying water all around in a funny payback attempt.

The teacher then threw the small boy over his shoulder, throwing him headfirst into the water. The boy and I grabbed the teacher and tried to push him under the water. Laughing and squirming as the teacher kept throwing us and we swam to him for more.

We played for what seemed like hours and I wanted to stay for longer, but the teacher indicated to me that it was time to return. We followed him back to the rocky opening and we found ourselves again in the lake, it now seemed so small. We came out of the water at the same place we had started our adventure.

"You better go, you will be late for school," my teacher told me with a smile. On hearing his words, I found myself wide-awake in bed. I looked at the clock and realized I had better get ready for school.

I didn't see the teacher at school that day, yet the following day I did see him. I looked at him and smiled. He looked miserable and gone was his laughter and his smile that I had seen when at the lake. His eyes were dull and for a moment, I wondered if it was actually the same teacher who had taken the boy and me on such an exciting adventure just nights before.

The teacher hardly spoke to me the entire lesson and I decided to forget about the voyage under water. I left class and was heading down the stairs towards the library when I heard someone behind me. I turned around and was excited to see the teacher. It was confusing as a part of me felt like I was so close to him. We had spent hours together playing and laughing, and yet today he had been so cold and distant. I somehow felt like he was avoiding me.

I smiled at him, but he continued to walk past me. I wasn't sure if it had been a coincidence that we met on the stairs or if he was following me, but he left before I had time to figure it out.

I went to the small school library. It was the fun room of the school and tables were set up with colouring books, paints, and books where all the children could read or paint freely.

I painted a fish, trying desperately to capture the colours of the amazing multi-colour fish I had seen in my visit to the Spirit world. An impossible task, but still I had fun painting.

As I left the library to return to my next class, picture in hand. I was rubbing off the paint I still had on my hands, making a mess of myself rather than washing up proper. When again I noticed somebody behind me and as I turned, I saw it was the teacher again.

I stood still and looked at him, I was sure he wanted to say something to me but unsure as to what. He stared at me and was about to walk past me when he stopped dead in his tracks and stared at my childish painting.

He grabbed it from my dirty hand and inspected it.

"It's a fish," I said, stating the obvious.

"Very nice," he said, slowly.

"Yes, it is," I replied just as slowly. I was wondering where we were going with this conversation.

"I had a dream of fish the other night," he blurted out to me. Now he was almost falling over his words with the speed in which he was trying to talk.

I looked at him and as young as I was, I realized at that moment what was happening. My teacher was confused, he'd had a dream about me and a little boy swimming, and he was unsure what to make of it. He was being cautious with me yet wanted to somehow bring up the conversation.

This was all very complicated to me. I could have jumped at the chance to say, "me too, me too, I had a dream, and you were in it and the fish and the laughter." Yet instead, I looked into his eyes, something was wrong. In my dream, he had been laughing and his eyes had shone with joy. Now I was looking at a dull reflection of the man I had spent the night with.

My instinct told me something was very wrong. Rather than answering him the many ways I could have, instead, I smiled and very calmly, I handed him the picture of the fish. "That's for you," I said as I walked away towards my next lesson.

Later that day I felt solemn. I wasn't sure why, but for my young age I was very solemn. I kept looking out for the teacher, it somehow didn't bother me that I had seen him in the Afterlife. I was too young to see that as a big deal. What did bother me was the feeling of sadness I had felt when I had looked into his eyes. For some reason,

I couldn't get him out of my mind. Yet I didn't see him for the rest of the day.

It was not long before I was going home when I saw him through the school gates getting into his car.

"The teacher is leaving early?" I asked one of the older girls who was sitting with us. "Yes, looks that way," she replied as she looked over at him getting into his car.

Then the girls started to talk about him, and that's when I heard for the first time about his loss. Apparently two years previous his young son had died.

Suddenly to me it all made sense, that was the little boy who had been with us swimming and playing.

That day after school, my mum informed me we were moving. This was something that happened often with my mum. I never returned to that school, and I never saw that teacher again, in any world.

Strange experiences like this would follow me throughout my childhood.

CHAPTER 4

Magical Adventures

The Spirit world is a place of nature. There are no words that can justify its incredible beauty. It's a noise within the silence, an energy within the air, an aura around every living thing. It's a place where I constantly have to look and then look again, absorbing all the details before me.

It appears very similar to our own world but it's clearly the source of it, it's beauty in its purest form. If you have ever had an overwhelming feeling of connecting with something amazing, maybe when looking at the magic of a black sky alive with a million stars. Then that feeling is just a touch of what it feels like to really and truly appreciate the beauty of the Spirit world.

Along the Path

One of the places I explore most often when I visit the Afterlife begins on a pathway. A light golden pathway that cuts between lush green lands. In the distance, I can see fields that appear endless. Sprinkled over these fields are millions of amazing, coloured flowers including poppies, daffodils, tulips, lilies, daisies, and roses, along with many flowers I don't recognise.

To my left, there is another large field. As a child, I spent much of my visits within this field playing with the many animals that roamed around freely. Pigs, cows, sheep, and other animals lived happily together in this field, and it was a popular play area for my friends and me. Often George would appear and have to remind me it was time to return home.

Continuing along the path, I would often see an assortment of birds dancing above me in the airless wind. Birds of many colours, types and sizes that would light up the sky with energy and colours flowing from them.

My Hill with the Tree

I come to a small turning on the left and there the path ends, and I find myself walking on dark green blades of grass. This leads me to a small grassy hill. This is the place I visited the most as a child. This small hill is the home of a large tree, and it is my hang out place in the Spirit world.

I have spent the majority of my childhood on this hill with my Spirit friends. Often sitting under the tree telling stories and playing games. From there I can see how the fields reach out into the distance. Miles and miles of colourful fields, that are alive with energy, almost as if the land was dancing. The sounds, the smells, the views, are all breathtakingly amazing and even as a child I truly appreciated this paradise.

I sometimes visit a woodland. The home to tall trees that almost cover the skylight. In this shaded wooded area, there is a bench by a small river. Usually, there are various Spirits sitting on the bench. On the rare occasion, I have found the bench to be empty I have quickly run to it, excited as if the bench was some kind of prize to sit on.

Never have I been scared to be alone in this woodland. Once, while walking deeper into these woods, I heard music. I followed the sound and it led me to a waterfall, a small, gentle flowing fall. I have since sat by this waterfall many times listening to the music the water creates as it falls.

Blue Ice

Another place I have visited, although only twice, is rather hard to explain. I found myself in an area where the floor was made of large squares, almost like thick glass. Below the glass shone a bright blue light that was almost blinding. I am unsure if these large squares are glass or ice, but as I walked upon them, the light shone brightly up from below the squares, dazzling me.

Although this floor was huge, the two times I visited this place I somehow managed to walk away from the strange yet almost enchanted solid transparent floor area and find a grass area. Both times I stood on this grass area was the only two times I ever experienced rain in the Spirit world.

A soft, almost gentle rain, yet it poured it down. I laughed and danced in the rain in a way I had never done in my own earthly world. Dancing in the pouring rain was almost an uncontrollable action and I laughed in a way I thought I was somehow going to burst. Both times were exhilarating and refreshing, almost like the rain was cleansing. Whatever the reason for the strange floor and the rain, it was fun to be there. I have no idea how to get to this area so I can only wonder if I will ever return and if it will rain there again.

A few times when visiting the Spirit world, I have found myself on top of a mountain, literally on top of a mountain. The view from up there is incredible, almost like looking at a blanket of amazing colours below. Each colour transmitting an aura of its own creating another layer of colours. I often see a burst of energy appear and disappear instantly, like huge smoke puffs, filled with a rainbow of glowing colours.

However, apart from the great view, being on a mountaintop has always been my least favourite place. Only because there is never much to do there.

My Home

Other than the hill with the tree, my most frequented place, and more so now I am no longer a child, is incredibly a street! A Street much as we have in the earthly world, including a pure clear pavement. I first started to visit this street over 20 years ago and now it is one of my most visited places.

This street has rows of houses. As the street bends slightly, it brings me to a white semi-detached house with a small open front garden. I always stop at the garden, bend down, and smell the perfume of the flowers in the garden. This small semi-detached house is my home in the Afterlife. This is where I will be "living" when I am dead.

It has a white front door that I know is only for show, as closed doors are not needed in the Afterlife.

On walking into my home, it leads immediately to a long hallway and a stairway. In the many years I have visited my Spirit home, I have never once walked up the stairway to see what is on the top floor. I am unsure as to why I never feel inclined to walk up the stairs and have a look.

As I walk into my house along the hallway, the first room I come to on my right is a room with large windows. It has a huge white comfortable looking sofa, a desk and nothing else as of yet. The room next to that one is also almost empty with nothing more than a bookshelf and a few personal items, some of which I recognize from my own earthly home. I assume I am going to have to wait until I die to furnish my spiritual home and to explore it fully.

At the end of the hallway is a door that leads to my back garden. Just yards outside my back door of the small semi-detached home is an open countryside with a small river. In the distance, I can see trees and buildings of all sizes. I often walk over the small wooden bridge and walk within the fields. I love stepping out of my back door and finding such incredible beauty. This is not just my garden; it belongs to any Spirit who wants to spend time there.

Many times, when at the back of my home, watching the river and the ever-changing countryside and listening to the surrounding sounds of nature, a young Spirit man will come and talk with me. I have met him many times over the years, and we talk and laugh often. He is in his early 20s and for years, I always saw him in a motorbike jacket. He is good looking with jet-black hair. He has a movie star look about him. I don't know his name and I never think to ask, but we have built up a very close friendship. He is my neighbour on the left, the house attached to mine.

Although I am unsure if he is a Spirit who has passed or if like me, he is just visiting the Afterlife, still we have become good friends. For a while, I haven't seen him in his motorbike jacket. Instead, now he often wears a white T-shirt. He also has a light around him I had not seen before and sometimes he becomes almost transparent before me when we talk, as many Spirits in the Afterlife do. All these years I have been his friend, he has never aged, until recently when I noticed the changes in him, I also felt him to be older.

On the right of my house, there is an empty space filled with flowers and shrubs. There begins a new row of large, detached houses. Comparing houses in the Afterlife is not something Spirit do.

In fact, I believe I only have the house because my mind somehow needed it and I feel the Afterlife has reflected what we need and has created streets and homes.

I discovered some years ago that the house on the right belongs to my mother. It does not surprise me at all that we will be neighbours in the Afterlife. Since in our earthly lives we have been neighbours on several occasions, and we have a lifelong habit of following each other around.

I know when we die we take nothing but our Spirit with us. Our mind continues to work, and our Spirit continues to live but we take nothing physical with us, as it is a world of Spirit. Yet the one wish I have always wanted in my earthly world is to own my own home. I guess as a child I moved homes so many times that at some point I desired to own my own home. Even knowing this earthly world is only for a short stay and owning my own home would change nothing in my life, still it was a desire of mine.

As the years pass, I find myself becoming further and further away from my dream of owning my own home. Yet knowing that in the Afterlife I have a small semi-detached house with a garden of paradise out the back is comforting and exciting.

I'm unsure what I will actually do in my spiritual home once I take up residence in the Afterlife. My next-door neighbour appears to always be outside, and I am unsure if I will ever actually use the house.

PART TWO

THROUGH THE EYES
OF A MEDIUM

CHAPTER 5

Becoming A Medium

Some may dismiss my nightly visits to the Afterlife as nothing more than just one long dream that has been connected throughout my lifetime, a rather odd feat in itself. Others may believe that my random meditations are nothing more than a hyperactive imagination. My prompt travels to the Afterlife may be classed as me being mentally unstable or as visions from that hyperactive imagination.

However, I know without a doubt that my visits have been and still are very real. I know the difference between a dream and a visit. My random meditations are never intentional and are far from my imagination. In fact, I have quite a limited imagination in many ways. However, I am sane enough to realize my visits into the Other world may be hard to believe for many people. For those who know me, they will know I don't expand on reality.

I do understand though, that if I had not myself lived the life I described within these pages, I too may very well find my stories rather hard to believe. This is why I have kept my adventures very much to myself for many years. Growing up I soon realized that it wasn't the best thing to add to a conversation. Instead, I kept my most exciting adventures along with my encounters with my closest Spirit friends, very much to myself.

The one thing I was sure of was that the Afterlife was real. I knew it was where our Spirit lived. I knew with conviction, it was a place where people's Spirit return to once they die, or like myself, when their Spirit temporary leaves the body. I had no confusion about the Other world I would visit. I did, however, have a lot of confusion as to this world. I wondered why those around me couldn't see the same Spirits I could see. I wondered why people made a huge deal out of death. Why so many people assumed death was the end of our journey. Even at a young age, I remember thinking that I was different in the way I thought.

However, I didn't have a problem sharing my psychic abilities. Most people would gladly accept my childish love for the tarot cards and from the age of ten, I was happily giving tarot readings and playing around with my psychic abilities.

My Quest Had Begun

When my dad died when I was 13, I was devastated. I couldn't stop thinking about all the lost time we had wasted and would never get back. I had been living in Spain and had visited my family in England at the time of his death. I had been able to spend a much-treasured week with him before his unexpected death, although I felt it wasn't enough.

After my dad died, I felt almost guilty returning to Spain, returning to my sunny apartment. I was in my bedroom unpacking my clothes from my suitcase and putting them into my wardrobe, when I found a bunch of postcards. I sat on the bed and looked at the images of Spain in its greatest. As I turned over the postcards and began to read, I cried as I read the unsent messages I had meant to send to my dad.

I had written him a handful of postcards, but never once had I posted them. I was deep in regret and grief. I knew I would miss him for the rest of my life.

A few days later, as I was walking down the stairs of my apartment block, I saw a random Spirit in the hallway. Accustomed to seeing Spirit all my life, this should not have bothered me in any way. However, this day it did bother me. I stood watching the empty space where the Spirit man had been standing seconds previously and I suddenly felt a lifetime of questions arise within me.

I sat on the step in the landing as I thought for what must have been hours. I wanted to know why, if I could see random Spirits then why couldn't I see my dad. I thought about where my dad was now. He was in my wonderland, I somehow knew that without a doubt, but I wanted to know how I would reach him. Would I have to search for him? Would I have to ask George where he was? Would he know when I was visiting the Afterlife and come to find me? Every question I never asked came jumping out at me.

For the next few years, I wanted to explore everything I could about the Afterlife. I wanted my dad to visit me, to appear randomly on the stairs. I bombarded my guide Micheal with every question that came to me. Including the question as to why me, why did I visit the Afterlife? What was the point of my visits?

None of my replies came to me easily. Some questions took years for me to find the answers and some I am still asking. However, I was able to find my dad, and eventually I was able to find out why I could visit the world just beyond ours without the need of dying.

From the moment I started to ask questions on that sunny day, alone in the stairway, I never stopped asking. Often one answer would lead me to another question. I asked Micheal anything and everything. I kept a dream journal, and I questioned any random Spirit I was seeing until I found answers, but what could I do with my answers?

Sleep Waking

Some years later, I returned to the UK with my Spanish souvenir, my husband Andres. I didn't particularly adapt to my return home, although Andres loved it.

Just before my wedding, I wondered if I should tell Andres about my ability to see Spirit and about my adventures into the Afterlife. I thought long and hard about it and decided against the idea. I wanted him to love me, and I somehow felt that explaining my secret side to me might somehow put him off. I didn't want Andres to think I was weird, so I declined from mentioning it. Although I did tell him I had a certain sixth sense and I read tarot cards for a hobby.

I didn't need to tell Andres I was weird, he found that out for himself when we had been married for just a couple of weeks. One night I had a dream that I was in the Afterlife, and I was abruptly pulled back. I woke up startled and then almost had a heart attack as I saw Andre's face inches from my own. With panic on his face, he was shouting at me, "Wake up, wake up".

"What's happened?" I asked panic-stricken.

Andres sighed a sigh of relief and sat by me on the bed. He told me he had woken me up and I opened my eyes and asked him who he was. Laughing, he told me he was my husband, and it was time to wake up. Again, I asked him who he was and where was I. Andres said he looked closer at me and realized that I wasn't actually awake. Although I was looking at him and talking to him, he knew I wasn't really there. I hadn't known where I was or who he was. He began to panic, and that's when he woke me up for real.

I tried to brush off the incident. Although in a way it bothered me because I knew exactly where I had been, yet I had no memory of talking to him.

This happens regularly, even now after I have been married for over 20 years. Andres has become accustomed to me waking up with no memory and talking to him. It is still something that scares us both because many times when he has woken me, I have actually got up, talked to him, even left the house and have still been fast asleep.

Once I woke up fully dressed in the other end of town. I panicked and called Andres and he had to come and pick me up. He had no idea that morning while he was having a morning conversation with me that I was actually still fast asleep, and all I remember was waking up fully clothed at the other end of town.

Once I woke up at one o'clock in the afternoon, again fully dressed and in town. This scared the hell out of Andres because I had left the house at ten am that morning and he had not realized I was asleep. We still don't know where I went or what I did in those three hours. Andres has learnt over the years to be very careful when he wakes me up. He now knows when this happens due to the look in my eyes, and he will not allow me to leave until I have woken fully. We realize it's a kind of sleepwalking, although I am fully functional. The amazing thing for me though, is that it only ever happens if I am dreaming, I am in the Afterlife. Any other dreams and I wake up fine.

A Life Changing Night

Shortly after my return to the UK, my aunty Maxine asked me if I wanted to go with her to a psychic night. Excited, I went with her with expectations of tarot stalls and psychics. I was surprised when we entered a medium size hall that was lined with seats all facing a stage.

Unsure of what was about to happen, I sat next to my aunty in one of the many seats. A friendly looking woman came and stood on the stage and began a talk. Within half an hour, my life had changed. I couldn't believe it. The woman on the stage was a medium, she was connecting with Spirit and giving messages to people sat in the audience. I was almost speechless as I realized this woman, in a more evolved way, was doing just as I did. She was seeing Spirits and talking about the Afterlife, and everyone applauded her for it.

I gasped loudly as I was informed that the following week another medium was to come to the hall and give a mediumship performance. "What, there's more of them?" I quietly asked myself.

As I left the building on a high, I wanted to tell my aunty Maxine that the woman was doing what I did and how I also saw Spirits. However, I kept my silence, almost overwhelmed with my new knowledge that other people were also seeing Spirit and had made it their career choice.

A few months later, I joined a psychic development course with my close friend Kerry. I joined only because it said they did tarot classes on the course, and I was always willing to advance with my tarot.

I was surprised that the teacher of the group spoke a lot about Spirit and the Afterlife. I would always go silent each time I heard her mention her communications with Spirit, almost scared I would blurt out to her my own experiences.

Looking back, it was clear that mediumship was my life's work. Yet I was still sure I wanted to become a tarot reader. I was also aware that there was a huge difference between myself and the many mediums I was observing at the spiritual churches where I was becoming a regular. The difference was clear, they could pass on messages from Spirit to those who were living. I only ever saw random Spirits and never had I been given a message to pass onto anybody.

That began to change the more I started to develop as a tarot card reader. I would be happily giving a reading and suddenly I saw or felt the energy of Spirit. Often, I would hear a name or one word, but the more tarot readings I was giving, the more my messages from Spirit started to become longer and more intense. Once I had finally reached my childhood dream of becoming a tarot card reader, I realized that tarot was no longer my only passion. Now I wanted to become a medium. I wanted to be able to pass on messages from Spirit to their loved ones. I wanted to be able to show a person that their loved one was still alive, only in another world. A world just beyond ours. A world I knew without doubt was real and I was a regular visitor.

Walking the Talk

I believe now looking back that my experiences of the Afterlife were all part of my plan for me to work with Spirit as a psychic medium and to be able to share with my clients the wonders of the Afterlife. I would not be able to share my work with such passion and belief if I had not had a lifetime of experience to prove to myself that my work was valid and although I would never try to change another person's beliefs, I know I had to believe to be able to do my work.

Becoming a medium was one of the best times of my life.

Finally, my lifetime of experiences made sense. I knew that this was my path and my entire life had been preparing me for it. I really was my own best friend and I had somehow planned it perfectly. There was little else I could become other than a medium. It all made sense. However, I still had to learn how to become a working medium. I still had to put the practice and the time in. Thankfully Spirit helped me every step of the way.

As I put myself onto the road of mediumship, eager to learn. I met more and more like-minded people and at last not only did I find that seeing Spirit was normal with many of my newfound friends but it was also something that was encouraged and worked upon. I felt like my doors had been opened and finally I didn't need to keep silent on my Spirit sightings.

Almost

Still, the road wasn't made much easier when it came to the Afterlife. Surprisingly, I soon found that to see Spirit and to communicate with them was called a gift. However, to enter their world and talk about their world was still classed as somewhat crazy. I couldn't work it out, even some hardcore spiritual mediums seem to somehow stop on the subject of the Afterlife itself. Often, (although surprisingly not always,) the Spirit world itself was accepted as a glorious place yet talk about it was seldom and extremely confusing.

I couldn't figure out why seeing Spirit was a gift yet seeing the Spirit world itself was classed as strange and outside the norm. I was encouraged to see, listen, and communicate with a Spirit person who had passed over into another dimension, and yet the dimension itself was often a closed-door subject.

Again, I found my silence, this time a somewhat frustrated silence. I had one foot in the door and the other just hanging in the air.

The few times the Spirit world was talked about within the groups of budding mediums I was involved with, I kept my silence. As I listened to stories of golden gates, different levels and realms and burning fires of hell, I kept quiet as I thought about the brightly colored world of energy, love, and joy that I knew so well.

Hard Work

Ironically, it actually became harder to see Spirit when I wanted too more than ever. Instead, I began to use more and more a simple ability I used all my life with Micheal, I began to sense Spirit. I began to feel them inside my mind, I didn't need to see them fully, I could sense what they looked like and what they wanted to say. I could see and hear them inside my own mind for longer periods than I could see them or hear them in a more physical looking sense.

I also found that when Spirit showed themselves to me in full physical looking body, they would often disappear and leave me without a message for my quickly growing clientele. I needed a message to be the medium I wanted to be. It didn't work for me describing my clients loved one and then coming to a blank. I also found that when Spirit spoke to me physically, in my ear, I often couldn't see them or receive more than a name or a few words. It appeared I wasn't able to put the entire pack together. I couldn't see them physically, hear them physically and receive a message at the same time.

Instead, I learnt how to mix and match, sometimes I would see a Spirit fully and give a message that I heard inside my mind, other times I could hear the message in my ear and yet see the Spirit within my mind. Spirit began to give me important details about themselves, so their loved ones easily recognized them, and I was then able to pass on a message.

I realized after some years of work that Spirit wants the same as I do. Spirit wants to take away the fear of death and the grief of loss by sharing with their loved ones the truth of what it's really like in the Spirit world and what it is that they do while there. They want to tell their loved ones that they are still very much alive, just in another place.

I felt somewhat stupid that I had been hiding my knowledge for so many years when Spirit was trying so hard to give the message that I always knew that Heaven is a real place and that death is just a simple step forward.

Now I knew what my work in life was, I was able to help others understand a little of what I knew about the Afterlife.

At Last

Thankfully, it was working with Spirit that helped me find my voice and break my silence. One of the most amazing things I found about passing on messages from the Spirit world was when I heard how Spirit described their homeland. I found their messages to describe the wonders of the Afterlife were very much like my own and I was able to fill in my own missing blanks to the questions I still had unanswered.

I gave a reading many years ago to a woman named Amy, her Uncle Tom, whom she had been very close to, came through in Spirit with some lovely Spirit communication. Amy asked me what it was like in Heaven and immediately Tom showed me images of the Afterlife much like my own viewings. He told her about how beautiful it was and how much peace he felt. He explained in some detail how abundant with flowers, colour, and life it was in the Spirit world. Meadows scattered with millions of bright wildflowers that covered the ground with their vibrant mix of colour and filled the air with strong perfume. I immediately recognised Tom's description of the Afterlife. Tom then told me that even the rain was magical, always making him want to dance in the rain. He described the feeling of almost wanting to burst with joy.

As I passed on each message to Amy, she was slightly surprised it ever rained in the Afterlife. I was excited as I wondered if Tom had visited the same place I had when I had stepped away from the blue ice or had it rained somewhere else. I couldn't really ask as Amy's messages were more important than my own enquiries and at the time, I didn't know how to do both, but I thought it was exciting how Tom had also danced under the rain.

I realised I had something in common with Spirit. They could enter my world just as I entered theirs and by being a medium, I was able to connect and understand even more, the place I once called home.

CHAPTER 6

Fields Of Gold

As a child, I was accustomed to seeing fields covered with layers of yellow flowers in the Afterlife. I often saw the ground twinkle with shining little diamond type lights, creating a glimmering effect amongst the colours. I would run and play within the yellow fields as any child would. I ran after butterflies as they almost teased me in their games and I would lie on the grass, fascinated by the slow movement of a caterpillar. I would always seek out any animal and ladybugs, ants, birds, dragonflies and even flies became part of my journey in the Spirit world. I am always excited when Spirit talk to me about these fields. Showing me, I am not the only person who visits these amazing fields.

Albert

One hot winter's day I gave a reading for a Spanish woman whose son came through to me in Spirit. The Spirit of Albert spoke to me loud and clear. Albert was born with a very destructive illness. One of the first things Albert showed me were that his hands were straight again and that he was now able to stand again. As Albert showed me this, I held my own hands up and outstretched them on impulse, almost like I had been clenching them and now I was able to release them and hold them straight.

As his mother saw me do that action, she knew without doubt that Albert was communicating with me. She told me that Albert had been unable to use his hands fully because his illness had twisted them, and they had been almost clenched shut. Albert was showing his mother that in the Spirit world he was no longer disabled. He also showed me that his mother only ever put one shoe on him, his mother smiled and informed me that the reason was that Albert, due to his illness, had his leg amputated some time before his passing.

Albert had a very hard life, suffering with an illness that eventually took his life at the mere age of 25. His parents had been left childless and heartbroken. Albert had been confined to a wheelchair throughout his life and had such an illness he had needed help with every activity his daily life required.

Albert expressed how grateful he was to his mother for all the work she and his father had done to help keep his life as comfortable as possible.

Albert showed me he had left his mother a legacy. I could not work out what this legacy was. He then showed me an image of a book, yet the image I was seeing made no sense to me, as Albert had clearly been very disabled. I was confused as I was unsure as to how Albert could write a book. How closed minded was I?

His mum confirmed that actually, Albert had left a legacy, he had learnt how to use the computer with methods that were way beyond my abilities, and he had written a book about his illness.

In his book, Albert had been honest enough to talk about his pain in a way that no one had known. Albert had loved his mum so much he had hidden his real pain from her all his life and only through his book when he had passed did, she realize how much he had physically suffered.

To me it seemed a bit cruel, until both his mother and Albert told me, almost simultaneously, that the intention of the book was to help others who had the same illness as Albert, enabling other parents to know the truth of the pain this illness can produce. His mother explained to me that although the book was heart-wrenching for her to read, it was also very helpful for such an unknown illness.

His mother told me Albert's book had been written with heart and intention. Not to upset other mothers who had children who suffered the same illness as Albert, but instead to help inform them of things that may help their children live a more comfortable life and hopefully avoid the pitfalls Albert had experienced, that eventually cost him his leg and his life. It seemed logical and heart-warming once I had it explained to me in more detail.

I couldn't imagine my client's lifetime of emotions. Caring for her son who from birth had lived with his illness. Not only had she helplessly watched him die, but also, she then read about the true extent of his pain, page by page.

Albert told me some smaller details about his life and the people in it, he showed me a picture his mother had of him in a scarf that they had bought when they had been on holiday to Benidorm, and he spoke to me about a girl he liked.

Albert then told me that now he had passed to the Spirit world his work was to help find a human cure for the illness he had endured when he was alive.

"Can't you just think of a cure?" I asked him rather naively yet with genuine interest about how such a thing would come about. Albert explained to me that it was not as simple as that. He jokingly told me he was dead not a genius. He also told me that the hard part was not the cure itself, it was to guide the right people in the right direction to creating the cure in the physical world.

He had to guide somehow, the right doctor to think the right thoughts who would meet the right person who would have the means of funding, etc. etc. It was as if a precise plan on how to get this cure into the world had to be put into place by guiding those in this world.

Albert explained he couldn't just take a cure, throw it into the sea of earth, and hope the right person picked it up. There was a very highly evolving plan put into motion. Albert explained he was part of an entire team of Spirits that were all working together to help with this cure.

For some reason, I felt without a doubt that Albert was the Spirit that could do this, and I knew that in my lifetime I would one day hear about a breakthrough with a new cure for this illness.

Albert's mother asked me if Albert was happy in the Spirit world. Albert instantly showed me a very clear image of himself, he was walking in fields of yellow flowers. I then saw an image of him with a dog and Albert was running in the fields with his dog, stopping only to roll around amongst the flowers and play with his beloved animal friend. He was free and was running and jumping and his dog barked and ran along with him.

I saw how Albert picked up a ball and threw it far out in front of him and both he and his dog then ran within the bright golden fields laughing and playing. I was seeing a glimpse of the life Albert was now living. He was making up for all his missed childhood. Every ball he could never run after, every dog walk he was unable to take. He was now making up for it all in the Spirit world.

His mum cried as she told me that when Albert had died, his dog had sat for almost two months outside Albert's bedroom door, until finally he closed his eyes and joined Albert in the Spirit world. The dog I had described to his mum was the same dog.

I was happy that Albert was living such a full happy Afterlife, but on the inside my heart was crying. I couldn't imagine what life he had lived, with an illness that disabled him more each day, year after year. The pain his parents had to endure to look after him the best way they could and to watch their only child cry in pain with the minimum of basic movement. Then to have him die at 25 and his dog follow him just two months later.

I wondered to myself, was this really the life Albert had written for himself? Had his mother really co-written such a life? It was as if Albert had read my thoughts and in that instant both his mother and Albert showed me, the small things that they had both took so much pleasure in. His mother started to talk to me about all the wonderful moments that they had cherished together, how a pain free day was a celebration in their home. Moments they had shared together of a gentle touch, a smile, a look, a kiss, captured in their hearts forever. Everything most people took for granted daily was special and treasured for Albert and his family.

Albert showed me that his disability had helped him to feel other people in a way I had overlooked. How he lived in a physical world so different from my own. In a strange way, they were both showing me not just the pain of Albert's life, but the private joy the family shared behind the illness. How everything I took for granted, no matter how grateful I am, everything I took for granted was all the treasures of life. For Albert and his mother, the small tender moments in life, was true living. I had been suffering financial stress at the time and after this reading, yet again, I put my life into perspective

Albert reminded me that when we leave our earthly bodies all illness, disease or disabilities are also discarded with our bodies. We suffer no pain because we have no physical body to do so. Our Spirit is a whirlwind of healthy energy that can never be destroyed, damaged, or sickened. When we reach the Spirit world, we literally can walk in fields of gold.

Polly

I gave a reading for an Irish woman named Shonagh. Her mother Polly, who was in Spirit came through and wanted to tell her daughter that she was well and at peace in the Afterlife. Polly was concerned about her daughter, and she told me she wanted Shonagh to move forward and live her life to the fullest.

Polly told me that her daughter had to find peace with her death and let her mum see her laugh again. It was clear that both Shonagh and Polly had been very close in life and Polly's death had devastated the family. Leaving an empty space where once had been a vibrant woman, mother, and wife. Yet Polly wanted her daughter to understand that she was still with her, she was still around, and she still loved her as always.

Polly talked about her funeral, an exceptionally special song had been played and Polly explained she had listened to the song when attending her own funeral and she was over the moon with the song. Shonagh confirmed to me that there had been a special song played at her mother's funeral and it had a huge significance that Polly had come through and had acknowledged it.

Polly also gave other details, small details to others but for Shonagh it was proof that her mother was around. Polly told me that her daughter was having dental treatment and she wanted Shonagh to know she was with her during the dental visits.

Shonagh confirmed that she was having dental treatment. Polly also showed me that the ring Shonagh was wearing was her ring and she was glad her daughter wore it.

Shonagh gently clasped the ring as she confirmed it had been her mothers.

"Is she happy?" Shonagh asked me rather seriously.

I then told her what her mother showed me in detail.

Polly showed me that in the Afterlife, she liked to visit a place that was beside a beautiful waterfall of many colours. This waterfall was in the countryside, and yellow flowers covered the ground.

I saw a sea of yellow flowers like those that I had only ever seen on my visits to the Afterlife. Polly then showed me that in these fields were dogs and horses and Polly would spend endless timeless periods with the animals. This was where Polly was the happiest. This is where she had found her peace.

Shonagh confirmed her mother loved animals, horses and dogs were among the animals she loved, and it made sense to Shonagh that her mother would choose to spend lots of time in these fields of gold.

Meadows in The Midst

It was no wonder Reyes was still mourning her mother's death. While I gave Reyes a reading the Spirit of her mother came through and wanted to tell Reyes how much she loved her and how she was still around, watching over her daughter.

Reyes burst into streams of tears, a well-dressed, very pretty, Spanish woman, with shoulder blond hair and dark hazel eyes. I understood Reyes was releasing many built-up feelings and her mother in Spirit explained to me why.

After her mother's death, Reyes relationship with her family changed dramatically. A lot of bad stuff happened and basically, Reyes was left with no family. Her mother told me she was with her daughter, by her side while she witnessed all the wrong doings that were happening since her death. She then informed me that Reyes father was going to die soon. He was on the last journey of his life and the mother would be there to take him over to the Spirit world. The Spirit mother also told me that she did not want Reyes to attend her father's funeral.

I was mortified, how could I repeat such a harsh message "Hey your dad is going to die and don't bother with his funeral." The mother showed me it was to protect Reyes and she showed me clearly that at the funeral, bridges wouldn't be mended. Instead, the presence of Reyes at her father's funeral would be turned against her and she would be highly criticized and made to feel even worse.

The mother told me she wanted Reyes to return to Benidorm on the day of the funeral, where her father had lived in his early days, far away from their own town. Reyes mother suggested that Reyes would be far happier if she was to go to the big church overlooking the sea and to sit and say her own goodbye to her father. The mother told me she was suggesting this idea because she knew that's what would make Reyes happy and it would keep her away from more family trouble ahead.

I passed on the message almost word for word. Reyes became silent and the tears stopped as I spoke. When I had finished, she wiped her eyes and sat up straight. Then she looked and me and gave me a half smile and very slowly she explained to me that for a long time she had suffered thinking about her father's death and his funeral. "I know it may sound strange, but I really panicked every time I thought about his death and attending his funeral, sitting with all those who have caused me so much pain. I am not ready to be alone with them all together," as she explained this to me, I understood. She then continued, "I thought to myself, I would love to deal with my dad's death alone, maybe go to Benidorm for a few days and sit in the big church by the sea."

It appears her mother's message was just one to confirm her daughter was doing the right thing and Reyes took much comfort knowing she was making the right decision about the funeral.

Reyes then asked me if her mother was happy. Immediately I was showed an image so clear and so big the only way I can explain it was as if a huge projector screen had started playing in my mind. Reyes mother clearly showed me she was happy and at peace, she showed me she had a lot of company, Spirits she had loved and lost were with her and she had a busy life. She showed me she is often by Reyes side, watching out for her.

Then she showed me she spends a lot of time in the meadows. I saw images of huge meadows filled with vibrant wildflowers of all colours. I could see several huge dramatic trees in the distance. The sky was a baby blue, and the grass was long and wispy almost like golden corn colour hay. The images I was seeing were spectacular and Reyes mother told me that these fields were a place where she visited often. She also told me that when she takes Reyes father over to the Spirit world, she would be taking him often to these meadows, so he could find his own peace. Reyes took great comfort in knowing her mother was walking amongst these spectacular meadows.

Spirit, much like us, don't spend all their time in one place. In fact, Spirit has shown me repeatedly how very busy they actually are. I love hearing from Spirit about things they love to do and places they love to visit. The visits they show me of the fields are pleasing to hear about because I have seen them myself and I know they truly are as breath taking as they show them to me.

Daddy and the Daffodils

Some years ago, upon visiting the Spirit world, I found myself walking in a field of daffodils, millions of daffodils danced around me. As I walked along a small pathway in the midst of the daffodils, in the distance I could see a man. As I walked forward along the path, I realized it was my own dad.

I have missed him so much since his death and before, and even though I know he is in the Spirit world, even though I know he is happy, it doesn't stop me from missing him in my life. I missed him more than ever when I had my children. I wondered what kind of Granddad he would have been. I missed him as I grew into a woman, when I wrote my first book and at every event where a dad should be by her daughter's side. Although I am lucky, as I know he is living his life in the Afterlife to the fullest. I know he is with me in Spirit and stands by my side often to share my life, yet I am selfish enough to wish he were still in my earthly life.

This day I was seeing him as clear as daylight, the sun was shining around him giving him an almost Angelic appearance as he shone in the light. The many daffodils danced around me almost as excited as I was and yet I knew he was too far away from me. I knew I wouldn't quite reach him, and I didn't. Instead, I left the daffodil fields and returned to my own world. It was shortly afterwards that I found out my dad's ashes had been scattered over daffodils. I like to think of him in his field of gold.

CHAPTER 7

The Sound of Music

The silence of the Afterlife was always something as a child I loved, it was almost like a happy silence. However, if I stopped for one moment and listened, the entire place is abundant with music.

Once, while there, I was sitting by a lake, and I started humming along to music I could hear in the distance. I began to search for the source of the music. I looked all around me, and I found no source of the music. I remember being puzzled as to where such wonderful music was coming from and like most things, the more I noticed something the more it appeared to happen, in this case, the music was becoming louder and louder.

As a child, I grew up listening to my Granddad play the piano, I also heard my mum singing at almost any chance she had. My mum has a beautiful voice and I used to love to hear her sing. My mum also tried her hand at the guitar and keyboard. Often, I would come home from school to hear my mum singing along to her records or playing the keyboard.

Music constantly played wherever I was as a child. When I was at my Nana's, my aunty Janet would play all her classical songs and I learned a great love for classical music, almost as if she was able to transmit her passion to me. My cousin Amanda always had modern music playing and we would both dance for hours and my cousin Luke on my dad's side of the family was a budding musician who played many instruments, I loved watching him practice.

I myself am completely tone deaf. In fact, as a child, when I realized that I could not play the violin, I swore it was not my fault and convinced my mum to buy me a new violin. On realizing that in fact, it wasn't the instrument's fault, instead it was me who couldn't quite get the grasp of it, I decided to quit and instead I opted for something I thought was simpler, like the piano. I was asked kindly not to return to piano lessons. I was also advised not to return to drum lessons, guitar lessons and even flute class told me I was wasting their time.

I decided instruments didn't like me, so I joined the choir, it was an embarrassing day for me as a young girl to be told not to return to choir classes, as I was tone deaf.

I have never played another instrument since nor have I ever sung again in public, thankfully.

The music was becoming louder and louder and as I listened to the music by the water, I lay down on the grass and as the heat of the sun basked my body. I found myself listening to the waves of music. I knew the music was coming from the water, it had an almost chime around it, something I had heard a few times when I had been around water in the Spirit world. I lay back and as my head gently touched the green grass, I could hear the grass almost singing back to the water. Obviously, I can't describe sound, but I can say that it was like a perfect harmony of water and grass creating music.

From that day onwards, I opened my heart to the music of the Other world and I have heard it pouring out of nature in a truly marvellous wave of sound.

In my own world, I love the sound of the waves hitting the shorelines of the beach, I have been blessed for many years as I have been able to live in places directly in front of the sea and the sound of waves has been the soundtrack of my life.

Although I have heard no sounds in this world that compares to the perfect harmony of nature that surrounds the Afterlife, nature is the noisiest sound I ever heard.

When I am in the Spirit world, I can almost hear the flowers growing. The tinkle high tune of a waterfall gently gliding down the musical scale as it hits the water below. In turn, the water plays gently with the surrounding rocks, creating the lower pitch tone of the scale, the grass almost sings as it grows and the more I have stopped in silence to listen to the buzzing noise of nature the more I have heard how everything, from a single grain of grass to the biggest mountain. Everything in the Spirit world has a musical note, everything is alive with the sound of music and amazingly, when I am in the Afterlife, I am no longer tone deaf!

Spirit also love the sounds of nature from their world. Often, they have lightly touched on the topic when I have been communicating with them. As if the wonderful tunes of musical notes that can be heard from the nature of the Afterlife isn't enough, Spirit also have instruments and singing to create even more sound. I found this out after years of giving readings where Spirit have often mentioned their favourite songs from when they were alive, and I realised that Spirit still enjoyed the same songs when in the Spirit world. Often Spirit come close to a loved one when they play the songs they liked when alive.

Spirit have also mentioned to me about their own music from the Other side. Often it has been explained to me how Spirit are constantly creating music, how they play instrument's and how they sing.

Becoming Music

The Spirit of Miriam, a young Spanish woman who passed due to an accident, came through to me in a reading I was giving to her sister. Her sister, Emily, had been devastated by the news of Miriam's traffic accident and the grief had been even harder because Miriam had been in her car on her way to visit Emily when the accident occurred. Miriam had just bought a new outfit and matching shoes for an upcoming wedding when she phoned Emily excitedly to tell her about her bargain finds and said she was on her way to Emily's house to ask her sister for her opinion on her new outfit.

Miriam never reached her sister's house. Instead, a car had collided head on with hers and she was killed instantly. Miriam was buried in her new dress and new shoes that had been saved from the wreckage.

During the reading, Miriam gave me many messages for her beloved sister. One of the messages was that she loved Emily's music and would often sit close to Emily as she played. Emily confirmed to me that she was a musician and since Miriam's death playing music had been hard for her as she knew how much Miriam had loved to hear her play. I feel she felt comforted knowing Miriam was still listening to her music.

Miriam then told me that she still sings. She told me that since her passing, she has been singing more than ever and filling up Heaven with her voice. Emily became excited with this message as she told me that Miriam had a wonderful voice and had loved to sing but had never found the time to do so when alive.

When Emily asked me if Miriam was happy in the Spirit world, I was surprised by Miriam's reply.

Miriam didn't talk about the fields of gold, the rainbows, the rivers, or the mountains. Instead, Miriam told me that she was very happy, she was living an amazing adventure in the Afterlife, an adventure full of fun and music.

"Music grows from the grass, it falls from the trees, it dances around me, I feel like I'm living inside a symphony of musical notes," Miriam told me.

Emily was happy that her sister was having such a good time in the Afterlife and that finally she had the time to become part of music as she had always wished when she was alive.

The Big Red Guitar

Edward came to me while I was giving a reading for his mother. Edward had died at just 38 years of age, after years of drug abuse and heavy smoking took its toll on Edward's heart. One rainy, cold day in May, Edward left his demons behind and due to a massive heart attack, he entered the Spirit world. Edward's first messages to his mother through me, was to say how sorry he was for all the pain he caused her when he was alive. Edward showed me all the anguish and despair his mother had to endure throughout the years he was taking drugs. Every day and night was a nightmare for my client as at any given moment she expected the news of her son's death. Knowing that one day that news would come, and it did.

Amongst the many loving messages Edward had for his mother, he also told me he was at peace now and that she could find her own peace since she no longer waited for the doom of the inevitable news. My client told me that actually in a strange way this was true. Since Edward had passed, she had found herself sleeping full night's sleep, the first time that had happened since Edward was 15, when she had caught him on drugs.

She was also able to relax when she was out, not wondering if the dreaded phone call would be at that moment.

Edward also thanked his mum for all the help she had tried to offer him throughout the years. He showed me all the times she had taken him to rehab, psychologists, and group meetings. Of course, none of these things had any long-lasting effect on Edward. Yet his mother at least felt good knowing that her son was finally seeing how hard she had tried to keep him alive.

Then Edward showed me a red electric guitar and told me to tell his mum that he was now playing the guitar, at last.

I told my client word for word what Edward had said to me. For a moment she stopped moving, she had been crying heavily into a tissue and now she had stopped crying and didn't move for what seemed like minutes, almost not breathing.

Then she looked at me and said she couldn't believe I had just said that to her, then she explained why.

Apparently, Edward had been given a red electric guitar many years ago. He had it hanging on his bedroom wall, no matter how desperate he had been for drug money, including selling his mother's gold and stealing her possessions, yet he had never parted with his guitar.

Often in better times, Edward would try to get his life together. His mum dragged him to rehab, and Edward tried to rebuild his life. He always started the new life by telling his mum he wanted to learn to play the guitar, that one day he was determined to play his red electric guitar.

As the years passed and promises were made and broken his mother realised this wasn't ever going to happen.

Shortly after Edward's death, his mother went into his bedroom. She explained it to me as a dark room with a strong smell of smoke, and there hanging on his wall was his shiny red guitar, a lost dream.

His mother sat on Edward's bed and cried, she prayed that Edward had found his peace. She also prayed he learnt how to play the guitar in Heaven.

Edward's words to me had shaken his mother. At last, she knew that her son had finally become clean, he had found his peace and he had learnt how to play the guitar.

Jerry's Gift

All his friends knew Jeremy as Jerry. He came through to communicate with me while I was giving a reading to his wife, Lyn. Lyn was a tall, blond woman who looked rather pale considering she was living in Spain.

She became emotional as I passed on messages from her husband Jerry.

"Your husband is showing me he is still a singer," I told her as I repeated the message I was hearing.

"He was a singer in life," my client told me.

Jerry showed me that in the Afterlife he still sings just as much as he did in this world. He showed me he was a regular at all the parties and reunions.

"He was a wedding singer when he was alive," my client told me.

I thought it funny that Jerry had continued to go to parties and sing, even after a lifetime of doing so when he was alive.

Then Jerry told me something I have kept close to my heart for many years. He told me that we are all born with many gifts. We are not born as one thing, to be a singer, to be a painter, a dancer, or a pilot. Instead, we are born with many gifts.

Some of these gifts will come naturally to us, like those who have never had a singing lesson, yet are able to sing. Others will be given the opportunity to learn a gift, and some will be given support to follow the dream.

However, that isn't who we are, we are not a musician, a painter, or an author, that is only part of us. We are all born with many gifts and opportunities or lack of, will rather enable us to work with our passion or to abandon it and close it up.

Jerry showed me that I was born to be a medium, as he told me so, it made sense. Yet he also told me I was born to spread my knowledge; I realise now that this is also true. He showed me that I was born to be a mother. I knew instantly that was a large part of who I was born to be, but he also showed me I was born to listen, without people to listen to music, there would be no music.

Jerry told me that we are all born with many gifts and to be many things. One of his gifts was to sing, he continued to do so even in death.

Lyn looked at me rather sulkily and declared that she believed she wasn't born to do anything, she had no gift at all.

"You were born to love me," Jerry said, bringing light on the reading. My client smiled and told me that was true, she had loved him like no other. Jerry also told me that Lyn had been wonderful booking and organising his events, she had a natural gift for helping him with the wedding bookings. He showed me how Lyn would often end up helping those who booked Jerry as a singer with other wedding issues, like the flower arrangements and decor.

Lyn thought about it for a while and realised that she did have a natural gift for such things. She then recounted to me that recently she had organised a birthday party for a friend. She told me it had been a huge success and she had felt truly happy at the end of the night, as everyone had congratulated her for the party.

It became very clear to us all before the end of the reading that although throughout their entire marriage it had appeared Jerry had been living his gift as a singer, Lyn had also been living her gift organising. She had never realised this before, always feeling she had been the shadow in the background.

Jerry then showed me that he was a big fan of Roy Orbison and that evening he was going to arrange it so a Roy Orbison song would be played for his wife.

Lyn was surprised at the message and asked me if that was at all possible.

"All things are possible with Spirit," I replied, believing in Jerry.

The very next day Lyn came to see me again. She had an amazing experience the previous night that she wanted to share with me. She told me what had happened to her.

She had been invited out for the first time in a long time and she was excited about going out for a drink and a dance with friends. After her reading, she had felt good knowing Jerry was not only ok in the Spirit world but that he was also still a singer.

She met up with her friends and they had arranged to see a tribute band in a large show bar. On arrival, she and her friends sat at a table by the front of the stage and ordered drinks. Two more couples asked if they could join the table. Lyn nor her friends had any problem with stranger's sitting with them.

Before the show started, the presenter came on stage and apologised. He explained that the planned tribute show had been cancelled due to illness, but they did have another tribute singer who was going to entertain them for a while.

Lyn told me she couldn't believe it when a Roy Orbison lookalike came on stage.

"He sang every song Jerry loved," Lyn told me with tears streaming down her face. Not only did she get the music Jerry had promised her, but also because she was at the front, the singer actually sang to Lyn most of the night, looking at her in a way Jerry used to do as he sang.

Although this was a magical experience for Lyn, the story didn't end there. The magic was about to happen.

After the show, Lyn had started talking to the two couples who had joined her table at the start of the night. Over general chitchat, the subject came about regarding parties. One couple had a 40th wedding anniversary party to plan and the other couple had a surprise birthday for their daughter to plan. Lyn quickly jumped on board and offered to help, and so began Lyn's new adventure.

Although some years have passed since the reading, Lyn is still a party organiser and is very happy doing so. I still hear from her often.

I believe Spirit love music; they love to play songs for us, and they love to listen to music. They love to watch us dance and to listen to the music of our world while also creating music in their own world. Music speaks to us on many levels, it's the heartbeat of our life, in both worlds.

PART THREE

WALKING THROUGH HEAVEN

CHAPTER 8

What Happens When We Die

Heaven is such an amazing place, a place where all things are possible. Any thought can become a reality. It's a place of pure amazement and unbelievable adventures. A place of fun, peace, and love.

Doorway to Heaven

So where exactly is Heaven? Well, I believe it is nowhere. There is no touchable place, no map, and no directions. Yet it is everywhere, reachable through the mind, interchangeable and parallel with this world. I have never seen it as neither up nor down, just there, surrounding us. The Spirit world is intertwined with the earthly world and the two worlds work in perfect harmony almost side by side. When we die, we return to being pure Spirit and with no body to tie us down we can reach anywhere we want. We can do anything we choose and be anyone we want to be with just one thought. I also believe that the Spirit world is more real than this earthly world.

What Happens When We Die?

On dying, our Spirit leaves our body from the crown of our head. It makes no difference how we die; our last breath is still a breath. Whether it be a long drawn out painful last breath or a just a regular breath, it's still just us breathing for the last time. Many people tend to wait until they are alone or at least almost alone to die. Death is a quiet and personal moment for a lot of people. If you have spent days by somebody's sick bed and they died the moment you went out for a sandwich or to put a ticket on your car, don't feel guilty. I am sure your loved ones were waiting for that moment so they could leave their physical bodies and return to Spirit.

Our Spirit then starts to make its journey back home. At some point, we will feel a warm comfortable feeling like sinking into a freshly made bed and about to drift off, or as has also been described to me, almost like floating in a warm sea.

Bright Lights

As our Spirit is filled with this incredible dreamy warm feeling, we see a light. Some have described it to me as a bright light and others as a bright rainbow of light, but it appears clear that as we leave our physical body our Spirit sees a bright light.

As a regular visitor to the Afterlife, I couldn't work out what was this bright light I was hearing about so often. If I could come and go without seeing any lights, then why didn't Spirit.

It was made clear to me some years ago that this bright light, or rainbow lights, is actually just the brightness of the Spirit world. The physical world is a dimmer version of the spiritual world. When Spirit shed the physical body and returns to Spirit, the first thing they appear to see is the brightness of the Spirit world. When they enter the Spirit world, it's like seeing for the first time again. It's almost like stepping out of a darkened room into the openness and the sunshine of the Sahara.

This dazzling brightness I myself never have experienced. I tried to find an explanation as to why I didn't see any lights. I now believe it is because I have been returning to the Spirit world since birth, so I am familiarized to that light. Although the fact that I'm not actually dead when I visit this wondrous land may also have something to do with me not seeing these lights. Maybe I see the Spirit world through my physical eyes and they somehow dimmer the brightness, although without doubt I do see everything so much brighter when I am over there.

On passing, as we step into the Spirit world almost like walking through a doorway. We realize we have no body; we look around us, almost as if a film is playing out just behind us and we see the final call of our death, our final scene. We may see our family members by our bedside crying, or the police and fire services closing the road and picking up our lifeless body from the roadside, as Darren did, a Spirit who I recently gave a reading to for his girlfriend.

Darren came through with a message of love and peace, but his girlfriend wanted to know if he had "felt" the car crash that killed him.

Darren explained to me that he had been listening to music on his car radio, and out of the blue a bike appeared. Darren swerved to miss the bike and the next thing he felt was a feeling of peace. He saw a bright light and was drawn to it. Darren described the feeling as almost like a magnet, not like an option.

He then looked behind him and saw the damage the accident had done to his car. He watched as police cars and firefighters arrived. He then saw his dead body just lying there, almost as if he was sleeping. He had felt no pain or loss. Darren immediately accepted his death.

Pick Up

Almost immediately upon dying, and many Spirits have told me that this happens even before death on many occasions, but upon dying a Spirit that we love and who has loved us will come and pick us up and "take us over." Although there's not very far to go, I get the feeling that it's a bit like picking someone up from the airport, it's to say, hey your home and we are here to share that moment with you.

For a long time, I thought it was nice to have a loved one come to us immediately on death and step into the Spirit world with us. Since then, I have found how important these encounters are, like with the Spirit of Bill. I was giving a reading for his wife and Bill was communicating with her through me. I was passing on messages Bill was telling me. His wife was concerned for his well-being on the Other side, asking me if he was at peace. Bill told me very clearly, what happened when he died.

Bill told me, that almost immediately after he took his last breath his younger brother who had died almost 40 years previous, appeared in front of him. Bill told me how his brother had looked so happy and at peace. In that instant, Bill knew that everything was going to be fine, he was so excited on seeing his brother he hadn't given his death a single thought.

Rose told me a similar story, she had passed with cancer some years previous, and her husband Joseph had come to me for a reading. During the reading, Rose told me that on her death their granddaughter who had passed some years previous, leaving the family broken, met her. Rose told me she was lying in the hospital bed and the next minute she was standing with her granddaughter by her side. She told me it was the happiest she had ever felt.

Spirits love to tell me who came to pick them up, for years I have had reading after reading where Spirit have told me who was there at pick up point, it can be a family member or a friend but always someone who we have loved. Often this knowledge not only brings peace for the Spirit on arrival but also for my client to be told someone close to them took over their loved one to Spirit. Joseph took much comfort knowing that not only was his wife at peace, but she was with their granddaughter. To him it somehow all made sense and he was able to find his own healing.

Party Time

Once we have been picked up and taken over by our loved one. We are then able to meet up with all our Spirit family on the Other side. Everyone we have loved will come to see us and throw us a huge welcome home party.

As those we love are mourning our death in the physical world, the return of our Spirit is celebrated in the Spirit world. From what I hear from Spirit, this is no regular party, this is the party of a lifetime.

I believe I myself accidentally fell, literally fell, upon one of these party's many years ago. I had been in Heaton Park in Manchester with my Granddad on a nice spring day, and I had decided to roll down a small hill where we were sitting. I would do this often, lie down and roll, I would laugh all the way down, as my hair would be tangled within the grass.

I had just rolled down for the second time and when I stood up to do it again, I realized something was wrong, different. I stopped and looked around me and I noticed my Granddad was gone, and so was the hill!

Again, I looked around me, this time I noticed the crisp crystal air, and I knew instantly I was no longer in the park, I had just switched worlds. I heard music and laughter and I noticed the noise was coming from behind some bushes, I crept quietly around the bushes and there I saw a huge party taking place.

There was laughter and dancing all around, everyone I was seeing was almost transparent with truly amazing colours emanating from them, although I could also see clearly what everyone looked like. I knew immediately by looking at the people that I was seeing Spirit people and I was in the "place."

I realized the "birthday boy" was an elderly man who was standing in the centre of the party. I stayed by the bushes, watching, and listening and it was while I was observing I realized it was not a birthday, it was a welcome home party. I wondered where he had been.

The elderly man appeared to be happy, almost ecstatic. At one point, this elderly man jumped up into the air and did a somersault and like a child he continued to jump up and down and to do all kinds of acrobats as the people around him all laughed.

I spent a good amount of time behind the bushes observing the party and listening to the music.

Now, due to what Spirit have told me over the years I really believe that day I somehow rolled into the elderly man's welcome home party.

Spirit have communicated with me on countless occasions about how many people they met up with since they have passed. Recently I had a Spirit man tell my client, who is his daughter. "There's more of us over here than there is back there," referring to the amount of family he had on the Other side compared to living relatives here.

Looking Back

Almost immediately upon death, we are able to look at any moment we choose to, any scene that is happening in the physical world. We only have to think of someone and our mind can instantly take us to that person's side. We can sit by our grieving loved ones for as long as we choose, a few minutes, hours, days, it makes no difference, as the Afterlife is timeless. Spirit can appear instantly wherever they choose to.

Tec was a Spirit man who recently told me during a reading I gave to his wife, that shortly after his death she said a prayer for him, an old family prayer that had a lot of meaning for Tec. His wife confirmed this as true and was surprised he had known this as she had done it only hours after he had left for the Spirit world.

Spirit can travel between worlds so effortlessly that it did not surprise me in the slightest. Although Tec had just reached the Spirit world and was reuniting with his family, he was also able to be by the side of his wife and watch her say a prayer shortly after his death.

In Between Time

Spirit can travel in an instant to not just places but also Spirit can travel in time at any given thought. If they think of a memory gone by, Spirit can instantly return to that memory and watch the entire scene happen before them. It appears there is no limit on time or space once you return to Spirit.

This knowledge was quite breath-taking for me as I realized that if once we return to the Spirit world we can instantly return to any point in time, then that means that our life is literately endless. At any point once we die, we can return to our past and see it all again. To think that in years to come, when I am gone from this world, I can think of this very second I am writing these words and again I will be able to see my life as I do now.

My son has just bought me an ice pop as the heat in Spain this year is almost traumatic, my husband is sitting on the sofa fixing something on his laptop and I am having a relaxing Sunday writing while also messaging my daughter. I am listening to the waves and can hear the laughter from children in the sea. This very moment, along with every other moment from my life has been captured like a film recording for the rest of eternity, allowing me to watch it whenever I choose.

The Funeral

Many Spirits I have communicated with over the years have told me in detail about their own funeral, being present at their own funeral seems to be something Spirit love to do.

The Spirit of Trisha told me that someone fell down at her funeral. Her sister, who I was giving the reading for, confirmed that the funeral was on a cold day and that their other sister had slipped and fell down at the funeral while following the coffin.

Lisa's mother told me that on the day of her funeral it rained as if it had not rained for years, Lisa confirmed the rainy day.

Madison told me that everyone danced at his wake, his wife confirmed this by telling me she was an Irish dancer and her dancing group had put on a show for his wake, and everyone who attended had actually danced.

I don't feel that Spirit attends their own funeral for any other reason than to be there to support those who are grieving for them and to be present for their last goodbye. However, it has been made clear to me that they love to attend their last big day here.

Popping Back

It's not just the funeral or the wake, one thing is for sure, Spirit love to be by our side. They love to pop back and see us; they still love us as they always did and they want us to be happy and to move on from their deaths as they themselves have done. Spirit are happy once they have passed over to the Spirit world, more happier than they have ever been and they know without doubt that one day we will also die and we will join them.

However, until that moment, we have to let them enjoy their life after life, and when they come by our side, it should not be just for tears, for sadness or for sorrow, it should also be to watch us smile, to see us dance, to participate in our excitement. They want us to enjoy every moment of our journey and to find our true potential even though they are no longer with us physically they are by our sides often in Spirit form.

Be happy and move on, is not actually an easy message for a medium to give, in a way I sometimes feel cruel on giving the message, like I'm trying to dismiss my clients pain and loss, and that's far from true. I myself am living and I cried buckets of tears when my own loved ones have passed. I have even cried many tears for the loss of someone close to my client, like when a mother who has lost a child comes to me and the reading is exceptionally touching with clear signs and messages.

After my client has left, I have often cried myself to sleep as I felt the pain, the loss, I am after all, very human. Yet I have to give the messages as I received them and when Spirit tell me to tell my client to move on and find joy in life, that they will be there waiting for them, then I have to give an honest message.

I feel like sometimes the only thing that keeps our Spirit loved ones back from true happiness on the Other side is when they come back to be by our side and they see how much pain we are in due to their passing.

This is not to make those who are suffering with grief to feel guilty, quite the opposite, I really feel that as living beings we have the right to feel grief for as long as our pain tells us to. There is no time limit on the amount of time we can cry or should suffer. However, I do know that Spirit work very hard to help us out of that dark place, so we can all move forward.

Maria had recently become a grandmother for the first time and her husband Derek who had passed some years earlier, had come through to me with some wonderful Spirit messages. One of the messages that Derek passed on through me was that he was so much happier now, he said for a long time he had been by Maria's side when she cried, mourning his death, missing him in everything. He tried endlessly to help her, but her pain was too dark. Now she had a new grandchild and he said he could see a happy Maria again. He said he loved seeing her with a smile on her face again, he laughed when she laughed, and he loved visiting her and participating in her moments of joy.

I feel this is what happens mostly with Spirit. They want to see us smile and be happy. They want to see us enjoying the life we have left. They join in with our laughter and our joys.

Mind Reading

Spirit know how we feel about them, they know the reasons we did certain things. If you feel guilty about something you may have done before a loved one passed. Maybe you didn't see them before they passed, maybe your loved one died, and you were not on good terms. Maybe you loved them more than anything in the world and you just want to know if they knew how much you actually did love them, then I believe, yes, they know.

I don't feel that Spirit are mind readers in the sense they invade your privacy, although I do believe our guide, who came with us at birth is able to read all our thoughts. I do not believe our loved ones know each thought we have. However, they do know the thoughts we have that concerns our feelings for them. Much like a phone line, we cannot hear all conversations when we pick up the phone, but we can hear ours. Spirit can see into our hearts and souls, and they know how much we loved them. They also know why we did things in a certain way, for good or for worse but they at least can see our reason.

Ciro was an Italian man who reminded me somewhat of the mafia films I had watched all my life, his square face and slick black oily hair only added to his godfather appearance. Ciro had argued with his father just weeks before his father's death. Not only did he feel guilty because he argued but it was made worse because he knew his father didn't have much life left in him. To say Ciro was consumed with guilt was an understatement. His father came through in the reading I gave Ciro and immediately he told me how proud he was of his son.

Ciro almost argued with me telling me that I could not be right, it was impossible for his father to be proud of him.

His father told him straight and I repeated the message. "You did what you did, I did as I did." Mmm ok, I thought to myself hoping there was more to this Italian's message then just that.

"I can see you on the inside, and you're good," his father continued. I thought the message was a bit lacking in words and somehow felt like I was talking to Rocky. Nevertheless, Ciro told me that was his dad's way. He said when someone did wrong, but was a good person, that's what he would say. Ciro took the message to mean that his dad saw that on the inside he didn't mean bad. It sounded about right and who was I to argue with an Italian.

Spirit Sanctuary

I just assumed for a long time that when you die any illness you have dies along with you due to the fact you no longer have a body.

This is true, but when I was in my late teens, I had given a reading for a young girl whose father had passed due to alcohol abuse, he had suffered severe depression for many years before his passing and his daughter and he had been on bad terms when he passed.

I don't think my client expected her father to come through from the Other side to communicate with her, yet it became obvious that she had needed to talk to him to find peace not just from his death but also from his life.

My client was a young woman with big blue eyes and ash blond hair. Her eyes filled with tears when she asked me "has he found his peace?"

Sure, he has, I thought to myself. He's dead, how can he not have peace? However, her father told me he was working on it. I was surprised with this message, and I asked the Spirit dad myself, "What do you mean you're working on it?" he then told me that although he had found peace and happiness he was still in recovery, a healing sanctuary for souls who die carrying mental pain with them.

I thought that was the oddest thing I had ever heard, why would Spirit need healing.

Yet since that reading, I have had Spirit show me on many occasions that they were in "healing" after death. It appears it is only Spirits that had suffered with the mind in life and since the mind doesn't die, I guess sometimes there is a need to heal a lifetime of mental confusion.

Joe was another Spirit man who had died in great mental pain. He came through in a reading to speak to his beloved niece, a middle-aged woman who was consumed with guilt due to not having spoken to her uncle in the year before his death. When her uncle tried to contact her prior to his passing, she refused to take his call. The next call she received was from the police informing her of his death. He had been murdered.

Joe had lived a dark life, not just with his dealings with others but his entire life had been covered in a dark cloud, he only ever saw the bad in people, only every saw pain and doom and gloom. He was self-destructive in life, and he had turned away any love and help he may have received.

Upon death, Joe showed me he entered the Spirit world as all Spirits do and he reunited with his loved ones. Joe then went to a healing sanctuary for a "while" until he found his peace again. I asked Joe to describe this sanctuary and he told me it was a bit like a hospital for the mind, only it was filled with love and laughter. He described how he was pampered and cared for each day, filling his Spirit with a glow he had forgotten he had. He was taught how to truly love his own Spirit and how to see the beauty of the world, both the Spirit world and the earthly world. He showed me that his entire being was engulfed in a bed of rainbow colours, and how the whole time he was at the sanctuary he felt the magic of the world that surrounded him.

David was another Spirit who also suffered years of mental issues here in this world. When he died, he found peace when his mother came to take him to Spirit. He told me that when he passed over to Spirit, he was consumed with a feeling of love that was indescribable, yet he then chose to heal so he entered the sanctuary where he was able to play for the first time in years. David described the sanctuary similar to what Joe had also shown me, yet David went into more detail telling me that the sanctuary was like a fairy story, it was a magical place to play and heal.

This sanctuary has been mentioned to me many times, the Spirit of Paula described it to me as the "happy hospital," and Paula told me she had gone there for a while to "get fixed."

Why we are not magically fixed the moment we die, I don't know, and although we have no physical pain when we die, to think that our loved ones who had severe mental issues before they passed can find peace and love is as good as it gets. I found it interesting that Paula and other Spirits told me they had chosen to go this type of hospital, it appears it is a voluntary stay.

The Spirit of Mary, who came to me in a reading I gave for her husband, explained this sanctuary far better to me. "I was so happy to be back in the Afterlife, but my mind was so tired, I just needed a rest." I passed on the message to her husband that she was now happy and at peace. Her husband said she had suffered bouts of depression over the years. Mary showed me she really was just mentally tired.

One thing that is very common when I hear about this magical sanctuary that heals the mind, is that people don't go there because they are in a dark place without light and desperately need to heal. Instead, it is more of a choice to help evolve and heal, it seems to be an addition to complement the good, not a form of rehabilitation or punishment in any way.

Judgment, Our Big Day

At some point in our wonderful Afterlife, we will decide to enter our days of judgment. Judgment day is a place we created based on the way we live our life.

At some point, we will stand back and review our life. We know that every action creates a reaction, and we stand back and feel each action we ever made, did we do it out of love, kindness or out of hate, out of spite, ego, or revenge. Every action we ever created in life will be replayed to us and we will feel the pure essence of why we made that action. We then feel each and every reaction we may have caused by that action.

It's too big to even begin to imagine in this lifetime how we could ever account for all the reactions, any after effects we may have left in other people's lives. It appears easy to think of the mark we have left on the lives of our parents, our children even our siblings. However, what about the mark we leave on the lives of others, friends, friends of friends. Including those we don't even know, messages we leave on the Internet, people we meet briefly in a shop or at work. Those that pass our life for just one brief moment in time and yet somehow, we leave some kind of effect on their lives. The thought of how many lives we can touch is so immense it is hard to comprehend.

This judgment day can be the only painful experience we will ever have once we pass over to the Spirit world. Even those of us who are good people will still have to feel any negative effects we may have left on the world.

If there is a hell, then our own self-judgment of our actions in life is it. I don't believe in the fires of hell; I have never heard Spirit talk to me about a dark place nor have I ever seen it. I honestly believe the only comparison to hell I can think of is if we do bad in this world then we will have a heart wrenched judgment day that may feel worse than the burning fires of hell that are described in some books. To feel every pain we may have caused others, deep down in our soul has surely got to be a type of hell.

I don't believe God or Spirit stand us up against a wall and punish us for our sins, we do that ourselves by living all the pain that we caused onto others, we do it ourselves by feeling in the deepest part of our soul every feeling we ever caused for others. Although I would prefer the idea of, say a murderer, burning in hell for eternity, I don't believe it to be so. Yet for that murderer upon death to find themselves in the light of the Spirit world and to realize that Heaven is a real place.

To come across all those who may have loved them or who they themselves loved and lost, to see the immense beauty of the Afterlife swimming in such love, to remember life before birth, life before their physical existence and then the shame when they meet their guide who they now remember clearly. The reality of the crimes they committed comes over them like a sickness within. There are no excuses, there is no hiding or running away. It's time to face the fall. Here comes their own judgment day, they have to look at themselves and feel the pain they caused to all involved with their crime. I don't believe I know enough negative words to describe how sad and painful this can be for Spirit.

We also feel the good that we did and all the love and caring help we spread around. It can be a magical experience as we feel the good times we created and the help we were able to transmit to others. Imagine feeling every moment of joy you have ever created in the world.

After the bad and the good, we also experience the unintentional and unexpected ripple effect we spread around the world. Often, we give out good or bad footprints without even realizing we are walking in the sand.

After analysing our entire life and the footprints we left on others, we then look at the effect we left on the planet, our holiday vacation home. We have to ask ourselves; did we leave the planet as we found it or worse, did we do something to improve Mother Nature's incredible world or did we blindly destroy it. Leaving the mess for future generations, for when we ourselves may return.

As you can imagine the entire self-judgment process can be a very colourful one filled with an entire spectrum of emotions. This process can take as long as needed, as there is no time in the Spirit world, I guess how long it takes doesn't matter. The entire process is something that Spirit have shown me they all do, although I have found Spirit to be rather careful in what they do tell me about this dark night of the soul, almost like it is very private to each Spirit. For something so grand, I would have expected many more Spirits to share information with me on this subject, yet repeatedly I find Spirit like to keep it private. That's fair enough, I wouldn't want to talk about all the bad things I had caused either.

Karma

Luckily, after we have judged our own lifetime, we are able to help somehow with the negative effects we left in the lives of others. Somehow, we are able to slowly cleanse our karma so to speak, cleanse our soul is the way I see it.

I know of countless Spirits that come to me in readings with the need to find forgiveness from a loved one, telling me to tell their loved ones how sorry they were for numerous different reasons. Although the simple words of sorry are only the start for Spirit to find forgiveness, yet sorry seems to be the message for many Spirits. However, I also feel there are other ways Spirits can help heal the world they helped create.

Like the story of Matt, a client who had come to me in quite a sorry state of mind. Many years ago, Matt had an affair with his best friend's girlfriend. Matt had been close friends with Tony for years and yet he hadn't given it too much thought when he found himself falling for Tony's girlfriend.

Tony was devastated when he found out about the affair between his girlfriend and his best friend, and it came to blows on a cold English winter night. The following week Matt and his new lover decided to move away. Having no ties left in the town, Matt packed his bags and took his new love over to Malaga in Spain so they could start a new life.

After being in Malaga for only a few weeks Matt realised he had made a mistake, it was clear his new love was still in love with Tony, her ex. It was also clear they were not as compatible as they had both thought while in the heat of their passionate affair. They quickly broke up and Matt stayed in Spain and his lover returned home.

It took Matt fifteen years to return to his hometown. He had created a life for himself in Spain, yet he knew it was now time to return. On his return, he asked around for some of his old friends but found he was pretty much alone, finally, he wondered if Tony had forgiven him, and he asked around for Tony. No one appeared to know Tony. A few weeks after being in the UK Matt came across a pub landlord who said he knew Tony. Excitedly Matt asked if he knew where he was.

"Tony's dead," the landlord informed him rather seriously.

Matt was shocked, he couldn't believe his friend was dead. He asked the landlord questions as to when and how Tony had died.

"Oh, it was a while back now, such a shame," the landlord said shaking his head. He then continued, "His best friend had an affair with his girlfriend, they ran off to Spain together, he was devastated and took his own life."

Matt couldn't believe what he was hearing, the following week Matt had to find out if it was true and sadly, it was confirmed to him. While he was enjoying life in the sun, his friend was being laid to rest.

Matt had no idea of the consequences of his affair, he had just assumed his girlfriend had returned from Spain and she and Tony had reunited. After learning of Tony's death Matt lived with regret and guilt for many years, the guilt consumed his life. When Tony came through in the reading, he was the one who wanted to say sorry to Matt.

Tony wanted to tell his friend he had forgiven him for his affair and that although when he took his life, part of it was due to the affair between Matt and his girlfriend. However, that wasn't the entire story, Tony made it clear there were other issues involved and that Matt was to let go of the guilt. Peace between the two friends had begun and lessons were learnt.

Tony said that Matt had to let go, he had learned from his mistakes, he had betrayed his best friend, he had lied and cheated, but Tony made it clear that Matt wasn't a murderer, he hadn't been the one who killed him. The best way to cleanse a karma is to talk about it and to release all built-up emotions and feelings. Although sometimes there are other ways people help cleanse their karma.

I was giving a reading for a man named Johnny. For many years, he had great financial difficulty along with suffering from depression, on occasion wanting to end his life.

He had recently been given an inheritance from his aunt. A huge house with land now belonged to him. He could not understand why he got this amazing inheritance, as he wasn't close to his aunt nor to his family. For years, Johnny had hardly spoken to his family, so he was surprised to learn he had been left such a gift.

I expected Johnny wanted his aunt to come through in the

reading and explain why she had chosen to change his life in such a way. Yet it wasn't his aunt I communicated with, instead it was the Spirit of Johnny's first business partner, Jenk.

Jenk had done the business dirty on Johnny and that was the start of Johnny's financial ruin and his depression. I feel Johnny was not aware of how badly Jenk had treated him, but he did know he had underhanded him and in turn Johnny had lost everything. Jenk had gone on to have a very fortunate financially stable life and Johnny had never recovered the financial mess.

Although Jenk was not taking responsibility for Johnny's current life. Johnny had to work his own life out. However, Jenk showed me he had seen all the pain he had caused and how horrific his actions had been, he had now chosen to help Johnny from the Spirit world, he was somehow behind Johnny's new fortune from his aunt.

Jenk's deceitful actions all those years ago had fallen heavy on his heart when he had his judgment day and now this one action of Johnny's aunt leaving her home to him created an entirely different life for Johnny.

Jenk was now able to move onto his next "victim" so to speak, to continue to help put his wrongs right.

It is not only the big things like homes and finances either. A woman from the north of Spain recently won a holiday to a health retreat. She was obviously excited and surprised at her win, she claimed it was just what she had needed after a hard year, and she assumed it was her mother in Spirit, who had somehow worked it in a way for her to win the much-needed getaway.

We were both surprised when an old school friend who had passed over years ago had briefly come through in her reading. Her school friend told my client how sorry she was for all the times she had called her names and bullied her for being overweight. The Spirit of her school friend quickly popped through to say hi and to apologise, she then smiled and said she wanted her friend to enjoy her gift from her. It was she who had somehow set up the holiday win and not my client's mother.

For some reason, my client thought it made more sense. She had always struggled with her weight and after being bullied, she had gone onto a lifetime of eating disorders. Now she had found help and was beginning to attend self-help groups. She had really forced herself this last year to heal herself and that is why she was attending a place where the competition was held. It somehow made more sense that one of the people who had bullied her and hurt her so badly was witness to how she was finally rising above it and helping herself.

Can a house or a holiday help us forgive a lifetime of pain? I don't think that is the intention Spirit has. I believe it is up to each individual to find his or her own healing. Spirit doesn't ask for forgiveness just to help us heal, they do so to help heal themselves, it is their karma they need to heal. We need to heal our own life, we need to be guided to our own answers, but we need to find our own answers, not have everything be shown or happen for us. Spirit can't change our life, only we can.

One thing I have learnt in this earthly life, a life of hard work, weight issues, teenage girl headaches along with trying to juggle finances, work, dinner, and dogs, is that only I can eat for me, only I can walk for me, only I can exercise for me and only I can sleep for me. If I was to offer a million pounds for someone to sleep for me it could not be done, two million for someone to go for a walk for me and keep me fit, it cannot be done. Only I can do it.

Although I can pay for advice, I can be guided in this world. Only I can make a change, only I can live my life. Only I can only accomplish the things I really need in life.

When I was having my own financial nightmare some years ago, I asked, pleaded, and begged with tears for Spirit to help me, reminding them I was on their side, I was working with them. I saw them and played with them, I even went into their world, surely, I had some kind of VIP. As my teardrops fell, day after day I realized that Spirit was not going to help me in my financial mess. I was all alone in my pain. Yet looking back, I see it was the time in my life when Spirit was the closest by my side, how they had gently guided me, not to the financial solution, but how to see beyond that. How they had repeatedly shown me they were with me, and I was not alone. Yet I had to do it for myself.

I have yet to reach a point of wisdom where I understand the why as to the way things happens. Yet I know Spirit do choose certain people they want to compensate for the hurt they may have caused, and all the rest is up to us.

CHAPTER 9

Behind The Curtains

There is a thin curtain that separates the two worlds. So thin it is almost transparent to some. The Spirit world has no time, no space and is not to be found on the map, yet we can reach it through the mind. When we die, we lose our physical bodies, but our Spirit and our mind becomes more alive than it ever was.

We reunite with our family, we heal any pains, we experience our judgment day, and we are able to help those we may have hurt and be by the side of those we loved.

In an instant we can be where we choose to be, by the side of any friend or relative, we can be anywhere in the world. Travel is just a thought away, and we put a lot of effort into trying to communicate with our loved ones. Spirits send us signs hoping we will understand them. Somehow, signs have become our new language and Spirit desperately send signs in the hope we will acknowledge them for what they are. Almost like phone calls or postcards, little text messages. Just to say they are with us and thinking of us.

Spirit are able to remember all their past lives of every life they have ever lived, they also remember the Spirit world before they were born into their last early existence. They remember the plan, the deal and again they go about living life as they did before birth, yet with even more experience, more memories, and more love than before. They continue to live life in the wonderful Afterlife.

Soul Mate

I don't believe we have a soul mate, not one person who we choose to be tied to forever and ever, that's an earthly belief. I believe we can find love that touches our soul, our heart, more than once. That's not to say everyone will have more than one love, some people meet their perfect partner, and they grow and evolve together, living happily ever after. Some people will find love and then grow out of it over a period of time, some will lose love to a dying relationship that was important at that time, and others will lose a loved one through death.

I believe that love is different in the Afterlife in the sense that it's not a selfish "your mine" love, I believe we can happily dance with all our husbands and partners, we can be just as close to our first husband as we are to our last. Love is about sharing and caring.

Iris was 78 when she married Bill who was 80, they had met at school, and Bill had felt something for Iris that had never left him. When still young, Iris met a man named Herman, they fell in love and married. They had a happy, loving family life for many years. When Herman became ill, Iris was devastated, and when he died, he left an empty space in her life and a pain like she had never felt before.

Finally, after only having brief encounters with Bill for years, he approached Iris and made it clear he wanted to date her.

When I gave a reading for Iris, Herman came through in the reading, he showed me how happy he was that Iris had found love again, how it made him smile to know that she was dancing again, she had gone to Italy for her honeymoon and Herman told me that she had many more holidays to come with Bill.

Herman also told Iris that he loved her as he always had and that she was not to feel guilty for falling in love again. He made it clear that he would be waiting for her when she herself passes over to Spirit, but she had Bill now and Herman knew that it was also love, just a different kind of love.

The same message has been passed onto me throughout the years many times. Spirit don't want us for themselves and only for themselves. If you had more than one husband, when you pass you will meet up with them all in the same loving way that you were with them on their passing. Spirits are not jealous, nor do they get angry when we remarry.

Kathy had found love again after her husband, Jonathan died young from lung cancer, left with a young child the last thing she had expected or wanted in life was to find love, and yet she did. Kathy had a friend named Bret who she had become close to after Jonathan's death. Bret helped her whenever he could, driving her to the supermarket and other helpful errands.

Although Kathy was now living with her new partner Bret, she couldn't help but feel guilty, like she somehow let Jonathan down. While I gave a reading for Kathy, Jonathan came through loud and clear. He wanted me to tell Kathy that he was happy she had found love again and he was happy for his son, at least, he would have a father figure to be his friend and to look after him in Jonathan's absence.

Kathy was young and attractive, and Jonathan wanted me to tell her that she had to lighten up a bit, she had to try to stop feeling so guilty for feeling happy whenever she was with Bret. Kathy admitted that when she felt too happy, she was overcome with a sense of guilt. Jonathan talked her through this feeling, and I feel Kathy left the reading with a sense of knowing she wasn't doing anything wrong.

I find with widows and widowers, guilt that tends to surround them when they start to feel for another person. It's a shame that many cannot see that often it is their partner in Spirit who helped arrange the meeting of the new love.

I hear many widows and widowers say, "it's too soon," as if they are somehow waiting to fall out of love with their partner who has passed. I don't believe there is a time, I don't believe we start to love a person less just because time has passed. What I do believe is that

Spirits want us to continue to live, to love, to be happy. If in their physical absence we find that happiness with somebody else, then they support us and feel our joyous moments with us.

Do Spirits Watch Us Naked?

For a Spirit to watch us in the shower would be pointless, Spirits don't view our body as we do physically, so they would have no interest in our skin and bones. They also respect our privacy. That doesn't mean to say that Spirits don't talk to us when we are in the shower or lying in the bath, or even if we are naked in bed. However, our physical bodies mean nothing to them and if we are the type of person that would be offended by Spirit seeing us naked, I believe they would respect our wishes.

The same also applies for when we are having sex or on the toilet, Spirit have no interest in us doing any of the things we view as private, and they respect the fact that we see these moments as personal. Spirits don't like to intrude on our intimate moments, although while we are in bed asleep, or just dropping off, Spirit often see this quiet time to communicate with us. However, when having sex, we are not open to Spirit communication and Spirit would find no point in trying to communicate with us at such times.

How Old Are Spirits?

I believe Spirit can be any age they choose to be, and they can also show themselves to us in any form they want to, not forgetting that Spirit have had many lives, they can easily show themselves to us in any one of those life forms. However, to see a large man with a big beard and be told it's your aunt sally is not something that normally happens. Spirit show themselves to us as they were when they passed over. They show themselves in a way they are recognised by their loved ones.

When I am in the Spirit world I see Spirits of all ages, from young children to the elderly and yet I am aware that their actual Spirit is the lights I see beaming from them. I believe the physical appearance I see with Spirit is just like a shadow. It's not real, they don't really look like anything other than the lights they emanate, yet the appearance of the physical body tends to surround them as if some type of shadow was surrounding them.

I believe most Spirits stay with the appearance, the shadow, of the age they were when they passed. Children will still be children in the Spirit world, they grow and evolve, and they return to being the wise Spirits they were with their new added lessons. The appearance of the physical body is just like slipping on an old jacket, it's nothing important to Spirit and to keep the appearance of who they were in their last lifetime isn't an issue.

I do know that this can change dramatically, the same as we can see a Spirit of a child who died fifty years ago and still see her as a child, although she will most likely be an evolved Spirit, we can also see Spirits who are an older version of who we knew, as if they had aged.

Camila's daughter died when she was just three years of age and yet Camila sees her daughter often, each time she sees her the age that she would be if she was still alive. Camila isn't the only one who can see Spirits who have aged.

It's so easy for Spirit to change appearances, to change shadows, with just a thought they can literally look however they choose. Although I don't feel it is of great importance for them.

NDE

What is a near death experience? I believe a near death is when a person physically dies or almost dies for a brief period, but not the planned date they are supposed to return home to the Spirit world.

Many people around the world have claimed to have had a magical encounter with the Afterlife during a near death, I can only assume that their encounters are much like my own regular visits. Glimpsing into Heaven often changes the life of the person who had the experience. I believe that any near death experience a person has was also written in a person's life plan. I don't believe a NDE happens by accident, even if an accident is the cause of the NDE.

I feel those who have had that life-shattering experience, have so because it was written into their destiny. For a lot of people, a NDE can change their life, it's a bit like a wake-up call. However, the benefits to NDE are not only for the person who has the experience but also for those who later hear about them or study them. I know people who now believe in the Spirit world and have opened themselves up to Spirit because they have known somebody who has had an NDE.

Many books about the Afterlife are told by people who have had these wonderful near deaths and have returned to be able to tell about their adventures, sharing their new found knowledge of the Afterlife with as many people as they can. If we look back in history, we are sprinkled with stories from those who returned home long enough to tell the story. I believe a near death happens for an individual reason, depending on what the person receives from the entire experience, but it is also for us to understand more about the Spirit world. The more people who can enter the Spirit world and are able to tell the story, the more people who will listen and for one moment get an idea of what it is really like.

You Can't Take it with You

No matter what material possession or title you have in this world, you can't take anything with you except the only things that you can't buy: memories and love.

The nice car, the posh house, that Rolex, nothing is going with you and when you enter the Spirit world any title or fame you have will also stay behind. That's also a good thing for the poor people of the world, hunger, debt, and the broken bed will also stay behind. I have heard people repeatedly say over the years, "you can't take it with you when you go," but I wonder how many who say this really understands how true it is.

Like millions of others around the world, I also have sentimental items that I am attached to and keep stored. My children's pictures, drawings they did when young, bits and bobs that remind me of something that will make me smile.

However, I am amazed at the amount of "stuff" people keep in their life. People like to accumulate things, expensive things, cheap things, all sorts of things. At some point, something may be useful, pleasant to look at or enjoyable to have around, yet when something becomes a stale "thing" just shoved away on a shelf or doing nothing in a cupboard then it seems pointless carrying it around with us in this world. Passing it on to someone who may get some use or joy from it seems like a good idea.

I gave a reading for Kate, a large woman with short white hair, her rounded face, sunken eyes, and pale skin, amplified the look of tiredness I saw in her. It became apparent halfway through the reading why Kate appeared so dull. Her husband Bernie had died some years previous and one of the messages Bernie wanted me to pass onto his beloved Kate was that it was time to empty the cupboards.

"Bernie wants you to know he has no problem cleaning out his things, he has no need for them where he is," I said to Kate. This is a message I have been given often from Spirit and I realize that it's not an easy message to give, the items of a loved one are often much needed for a person to cope with their grief, and I believe it is up to a person when they should remove their loved one's goodies.

"I'm not doing that," Kate replied to me, she was rather mortified with the message from her husband.

Bernie showed me Kate had kept everything, every single possession that her husband had owned, including things he didn't really like.

Kate admitted to me that she had been unable to throw away anything, she had kept his shoes, his socks, even his underpants.

What was amazing was that Bernie showed me his wife also kept all the things she had wanted him to get rid of when Bernie was alive. Bernie had loved war books and he had stacks of them all in boxes in the spare room, for years Kate had told him to get rid of the books. However, these same books had become sentimental items to her now he was gone.

He had boxes of bits and pieces he had planned to fix one day, boxes of seeds he was going to plant, it appeared Bernie was a bit of a hoarder and the house had always been blowing at the seams with things he collected and accumulated over the years.

It became clear that Kate was trying to keep her husband's presence alive by keeping all his possessions as they were.

Kate reminded me of my own mum, when her husband Rick died, she refused to part with anything, even when she moved home several times, I found myself helping her pack and move each box with care. It took her a long time to part with his suits and other objects that were no use to her except to remember. It took me a while to explain to my mum that she would remember anyway, she would never forget, she would never stop remembering his smell, the way he looked, the way he spoke. It wasn't really the object that reminded her, it was her own heart that kept his memory alive.

Kate was doing the same as many people do when they have lost a loved one, keeping hold of any memory she could, fearful that by giving the books away she was somehow giving away a part of her memory.

I told Kate that she had to do what she felt best for her, but if one day she ever wanted to remove Bernie's earthly possessions from her home, she had his full support, he had no use for them in the Spirit world.

Kate nodded in silent agreement, and I decided not to continue much more with this message, I felt somewhat cruel. Although I knew it was the message Bernie wanted me to pass on, I was sitting a foot away from a woman who was obviously in a lot of pain, and she wasn't ready for me to tell her to clean out the house.

Thankfully, Bernie must have understood my thoughts and he talked about other things, including Kate's passion for doing charity work. Kate had now retired, and Bernie continued to tell me that Kate had dreamed of organizing charities but had never gotten around to it.

Kate confirmed to me that she had at one point become involved with a charity, but she didn't have the time to continue with such work.

"Now you do," I repeated Bernie's words to her.

Kate gave me a flat smile and said, "Yes maybe." Bernie then talked about all the people he had met in the Spirit world since his passing.

"He's met up with his old friend Dick who died of a heart attack before he was able to go in for the operation he had planned," I said to Kate.

Kate raised her eyebrows, "never?" she asked me rather surprised. I thought she had been surprised because of me coming out with the name of his friend, A pat on the back for most mediums and not as easy as expected. However, it wasn't that which surprised Kate, it was because Dick was a very wealthy, well-known person. She was surprised that he was in the same place as her beloved, yet lower class Bernie.

I had to explain to Kate that in the Spirit world it doesn't work in social levels, in the Spirit world we are all one, we come from Spirit naked, and we return to Spirit naked. The rich, the famous, the poor, the unknown, in the Spirit world we are all equal Spirits. We only take with us our feelings and memories and the love in our hearts.

I slowly explained to Kate that in the Spirit world, we can think of what we want, and we can produce it with our thoughts. We don't need money to buy things. We don't need anything at all, but for fun if we choose something, like a nice home then we can produce it. We don't need to buy anything, yet we can think of what we wish for and see it produced before us.

"So, all this stuff I have at home, I can think it and get it again when I'm dead?" Kate asked me.

"Yes, although by the sound of what you have at home, I'm sure you're not going to want half of it," I said with a smile.

Kate burst out laughing, "It's true, it's true, I got a home full of crap that I've been begging to get rid of for years," she said between laughter.

I realised how clever Bernie was, by mentioning rich Dick, he somehow had his message understood by his wife.

Over a year later Kate came to see me again, she appeared happier and on seeing me she hugged me as if we were long lost sisters. "Look," she said excitedly as she reached for her handbag. She produced around thirty pictures out of her bag. Each picture was of her home, a stunning house, but I didn't quite understand why she was showing me these pictures. Then she showed me a picture of a small two-door wardrobe, on the doors was a man's scarf.

"This is Bernie's wardrobe," she told me. Kate explained to me that after her messages from Bernie. She had over the course of several months, started to slowly remove his possessions and give them to charity. Due to the amount of runs to the charity shop, she became friends with the manageress of the shop. Soon she became involved with the charity, organizing charity events.

While cleaning out Bernie's possessions she also did a clear out of her own things. She realised if she died then all the mess in her home would be left to her son to clear out, and she felt that was unfair.

She removed anything she didn't use or didn't need and all the sentimental things that kept a smile on her face she placed in this one wardrobe. Now she had a Pandora's Box to open whenever she felt she wanted to hold onto Bernie.

For me, it was one of the last pictures Kate showed me that

touched me. "That's my office," she said excitingly as she pointed to a picture of a large, lovely looking home office. "That used to be our spare room where Bernie stacked his books and other things, now it's my office for my charity work."

When Kate was cleaning out her home, she realised it was actually very big and she paid for it be painted, then she updated her furniture and said she felt like she was living in an entirely different home, she loved it.

Kate told me that she actually feels closer to Bernie because of the changes in her home. She told me how she spoke to him every step of the way, like when taking his belongings to charity, and buying the dream sofa she always wanted, she made Bernie a part of her changes.

"I spent some money, but hey you can't take it with you can you," Kate told me with a smile.

Who Will Love My Child?

Somebody who loves them will also meet babies and children in the Spirit world. A grandparent or a relative who will come to them to pick them up and to watch over them on the Other side. Yet it is important to remember that although a child may choose to keep their physical appearance of a child, they do evolve once they return to the Spirit world. They do regain their memories of who they were before birth and the reason for their life, and death. They may appear to us in child form so we recognise them, they may also keep their childlike manners to some extent. However, they will have the mind-set they had before they left the Spirit world for their short journey to the earthly world, along with any newfound lessons they may have now acquired.

On many of my visits to the Spirit world I have played with Spirit children and seen many of them, I believe we all have a child within us and when we leave this world to the next, we can still play as a child would play, no matter what our age.

Abortion

I have met many Spirit children that have entered the Afterlife due to abortion. I know that the messages of love and the fact they are still around and close to a parent is quite shocking and often saddening for some parents. I see aborted children just as I see any Spirit child who passed due to other causes.

Some years ago, I was told that an aborted child comes into this world knowing they are going to be aborted. I find the entire issue of abortion mind twirling. In a way, to say a child was aborted because it was part of their life plan somehow takes away the responsibility from the parent, and yet at the same time, this is the information I was told. If we plan our life entwined with others then we also plan our death, no matter when that is. I don't feel it is my place to enter into any type of abortion debates, that's up to each individual. The only input I can give is that a child who has been aborted is a Spirit, just like any other. I also know that many people who have abortions believe that it is just an empty grain of rice lying in their tummy and do not realize that the tiny foetus is a Spirit from the moment of conception.

Suicide

I believe we all enter into the Spirit world the same way. Those who felt this world was too hard or had other issues that lead to them take their own life, enters the Spirit world the same as anyone. I have met many Spirits who have returned home early, and they have all shown me they are in the same Spirit world as all Spirits are.

However, I honestly don't know exactly what happens when someone takes their own life and I am hesitant to talk about it for that reason, but I am aware of the possibility that those who have returned home early are actually on time. The day of their return being planned well before their birth as part of a bigger picture that is out of my own understanding.

I have also been shown those who returns home "early," go to a type of healing sanctuary to recover and heal their mind.

I do believe that those who take their own lives are not actually escaping anything by leaving this world. It appears that those who return through their own accord still have to face certain issues when they pass over. Death doesn't just solve all problems.

Help should be sought in this world and worked through in this world.

However, this is by no means compared to a lost soul wondering eternity in darkness, as we are often made to believe.

When Michael, (Mikey) took his own life, his family were devastated, he was only a young man and appeared to have a good life ahead of him with a loving family to support him. When I gave a reading for Mikey's mum Lizzy and his sister Joanne, Mikey came through with messages of love. He also shared concern for his family, especially his sisters and it was clear he had loved them all dearly.

Mikey had his reasons for doing what he did, however, he was sorry for the pain his family and loved ones were going through due to his death.

I felt an instant connection with Mikey, almost as if I had met a new friend and he came through as a fun, happy, loving young man. A part of me that wanted to shout at him and ask him why had he done it, why had he taken his life and put his family through so much pain?

Mikey was concerned for his family, and he told me he would be with each one of them always, watching out for them and sending them signs so hopefully they could all move on from his death and instead celebrate his life, no matter how short it had been.

He told me he would bombard his family with signs to say that he was still with them, only in a different way. He made it clear that what he did wasn't anybody's fault.

To see the pain in Lizzy's eyes and the sadness deep in the souls of the family left behind is horrific and although I can't and won't judge what Mikey did, but suicide leaves a dark road ahead for those who are still living.

However, I have never been shown any punishment or dark place for those that take their own life, although I can't stress enough how I feel that suicide is never the solution. Yet the old myth that those who take their own lives are walking aimlessly in the dark has been proven to me repeatedly to be just that, a myth.

The Darkness

I don't believe that there is a dark place where souls get lost or where there are burning fires of hell. I would love to think of a horrid place where the evil people of the world go to when they die, but unfortunately, there isn't such a place. The burning fires of hell are the self-judgment and the entering of a place of such immense love with shame of knowing and feeling each sin committed.

I also don't believe in dark Spirits, ghost, poltergeist, or any other spiritual being that is often talked about from a negative place. I have spent many years asking Spirit about the darker side of life, Spirit have always shown me that no such entity nor place exists.

The fantasy of hell, the devil and demons sound quite interesting and in many ways, it would make sense to have a darker side to the light. But I believe where there is light there can never be darkness, only one can reign, and I have been shown and told many times that it is the happy, wondrous world of the Spirit world that is for real. The darker evil side is spread around in this world, poverty, murder, hate, revenge, anger, along with inner demons of addictions, lies and sheer evilness is an earthly thing. All negativity stays behind in this world, never reaching Heaven and although the cycle is often picked up and created again by others, it is always an earthly energy.

Religion

Because I live in a mostly catholic country, many of my clients ask me about Jesus and religion. I don't follow any organised religion and I have never had a religious experience of any kind when visiting the Afterlife. I have never met Jesus or any other religious figure.

However, I would like to point out that my lack of faith may be the reason for that, maybe the fact that I don't believe in Jesus in the way he is explained to me, is the reason he has never presented himself to me during my visits to the Other side. Maybe I am not worthy of his presence. Why would he come to me? I know of countless stories of people who have had NDE and who have come back from death to share remarkable encounters with Jesus. I don't dismiss these stories as untrue; it's just never happened to me.

Maybe it is not part of my path, in all honesty, if I saw Jesus, even for just one second, I would be shouting it from the rooftops. I would be doing as I am now with the Afterlife, dedicating my life to share what I know. My books would be mainly based around the meeting of Jesus. Maybe that's another reason I have never seen him or had Spirits ever talk to me about him. Maybe my life is to be centred on the Spirit world and Spirits, not religion or one Spirit alone.

I have over the years, spent some time reading about religion. I read the bible, and other religious books with good interest, however, none of those books or the information within its pages were part of my own pathway to Heaven.

Obviously, I respect people's beliefs, faiths, and religions. In fact, I have met many people over the years who truly believe in one religion or another and although the rules appear to be different, it does seem to me as an outsider, that the core of all religion is the belief that there is something bigger than we are. A belief I share myself.

I don't believe there is a right or wrong. If I am missing something then I'm sure one day it will be shown to me, if it's not then I will have to live with missing it. I leave the door ajar.

What I do know for sure is that no matter what belief people have, when we die, we all go to the same place.

CHAPTER 10

Things To Do in Heaven
When You're Dead

I am constantly amazed at the things Spirit shows me as to what they do while in the Spirit world. Some years ago, a Spirit man named Antonio showed me he was on an earthly holiday with his wife, who was also in Spirit. I was amazed Spirit would choose a place in our world to journey to in Spirit form. Since then, I have heard of other Spirits who take holidays in our amazing world. Sightseeing and taking day trips to this marvellous planet. Although most living people cannot see them, I believe Spirit are here in our world often and for many reasons.

I also believe Spirit arrange to meet other Spirits to share their little trips with. A client of mine had recently been abroad to Italy for her son's wedding. Her father in Spirit told me that he had joined the family on that special day. He told me how wonderful it was to have seen his grandson on his happy day and how all the family had taken the flight for the wedding. He also showed me it wasn't only the living family who had adventured off to Italy. His own mother, his brother and a long list of Spirit relatives had also been present at the wedding.

My client laughed as she realized there were actually two groups who ventured to Italy for the ceremony, the living family who shared the plane with her and the Spirit family who got a free ride. The father also showed me how he had enjoyed Italy and he told me he would be returning in September. My client confirmed she had booked tickets to return in September and she was pleased her father would be joining her again.

Spirit are able to be by our side in this world with a simple thought as the Afterlife is just a thought away from the physical world. Just by thinking of being in a place Spirit are able to be there instantly and I believe they make the most of this ability.

Homes in the Afterlife

I'm not at all special by having a home in the Afterlife, in fact, I speak to many Spirits who also tell me they have homes in the Spirit world.

Joan and Her Mansion

I gave a reading for a man named Carl, his wife Joan had passed with breast cancer and many added health complications at just 58 years old. Carl wanted to know if his wife was happy in the Afterlife. Joan came through loud and clear and one message she had for Carl was that she wanted him to know she was having the time of her life. Joan told me about the many Spirits she had met up with since passing, her old school friend who had passed suddenly, and her grandmother who had passed the year before she did. She talked about the celebration of gathering and the love and peace she felt after her passing from this world. She also told me to tell Carl that she was a very busy woman and that she had a lovely home, almost like a mansion. Joan described to me this huge mansion in seemingly pointless detail. Then she told me it is "out of this world."

Carl was not surprised with this message. He told me actually it made a lot of sense to him. Excitedly, Carl explained to me a dream he had not long ago. He had dreamed very clearly and vividly of Joan, and he had seen her in a home much like she had described to me, a home similar to the kind the rich and famous have here in this world. He said he had woken up smiling, knowing that she would have loved to be in a home like that and his good-hearted, hardworking wife who he watched die a slow painful death deserved a mansion in Heaven.

I think we can choose the home we wish to create, and Joan wanted a big mansion. Carl told me that some years ago they had lost the family business along with their home, having to downgrade and move into a rented apartment brought a lot of stress for both of them. Maybe that is why Joan wanted a big home now.

Fanny and a Home of Her Own

I gave a reading to a man named William recently and his mother Fanny came through in Spirit, an Irish woman who obviously loved her son very much. She gave me many Spirit messages for William, and he was able to confirm all the details she was passing on to him through me. She then told me that she had a huge home on the Other side, a house like none she had ever seen before. "The most beautiful home you could ever imagine," she told me enthusiastically. She was insisting I pass on that message to her son, she smiled as I passed on the message to William.

William explained to me that his mother had spent years cleaning homes for wealthy people. She was a poor Irish woman who was so kind she would often work and instead of being paid, the wealthy people would pay her with shoes and handbags. Often that meant she could never afford her own rent and when William was a young boy, he remembers being evicted from one home after another while his mother worked her fingers to the bone.

It was when William became a teenager, he himself would stand up for his mother and insist she got paid cash for her work, but even still, many times they would come upon hard times and find themselves being evicted yet again.

Scrubbing the floors and washing the windows of huge homes while she knew her and her son had nowhere to sleep that night was very traumatic, for both William and Fanny.

William looked after his mother his entire life, never living apart from her, even when he married, his mother lived with him, and she stayed with him until the day she passed. "You did me proud," she would often say to him as William gave her the most comfortable life he could, making sure his mother wanted for nothing. It made him happy to know his mother was not only happy in the Spirit world, not only had she found peace and was able to be with William whenever she wanted but that finally she also had a home of her own.

My own mum has obviously chosen a big, detached home and I was happy with a small semi-detached, since it's free we can choose how we please. It does not work like here in this world where the more money we have, the bigger the home. Instead, we choose it and create it. Money, status, titles have no place at Heaven's door.

The Spirit on the Boat

Often it has been shown to me that coming to visit loved ones is not the only reason Spirit choose to spend time in our world. They may come to this world because it is part of their work, maybe they have chosen to help the world in some way, and they need to be around to do so. Somehow, guiding and helping the people involved to make the correct decisions, whether they knew this person or not. A client of mine had come to me to complain about a Spirit whose presence he felt often. He had felt the Spirit for over a year and although the Spirit didn't bother him, he was concerned as to who it could be and if the Spirit wanted to give him a message of some kind.

It took me a while to work out who the Spirit was because at first, my client's mother came through with messages of love and then his younger sister came through with more fun and lighter messages. I assumed one of these Spirits were the one who had been with him and told him so.

Yet as our reading was ending, I felt the strong presence of a Spirit man. My client couldn't recognise him, and the Spirit wasn't exactly showing me helpful information as to show me his identity. It was becoming hard work for me as I couldn't really say anything constructive until he showed me a small red book with scribbled handwriting and pencil drawings. I wasn't sure what I was seeing but the Spirit was clearly showing me this small red book, he then showed me this book was on a boat.

"That's my book," my client said, becoming exciting as I mentioned the boat, "That book is a project I'm working on." My client told me that he was "inventing" something for boats and he did so while out on his own boat. His ideas were scribbled down in a red notebook along with the drawings.

At that moment, the Spirit man showed me exactly what was happening. He had been helping my client work on this project because it was something to do with safety and it would one day be put into place and would help save lives. That was the reason why this man was with my client, helping him and inspiring him. I asked my client if this made sense and he told me that actually his project was about safety and that he had been working on it for over a year, since around the presence of the Spirit.

The Spirit had been with my client to help guide him on this important project. The Spirit man told me he didn't actually know my client in life, but he had chosen this project to help it into existence. I assumed that was why he didn't bother showing me who he was or what he had died from, my client didn't know him so it would have been pointless.

My client informed me of the ins and outs of this project, I know nothing about boats so he could have told me in Chinese, I had no idea what he was talking about. What I did understand was that the future of safety aboard boats was about to change in one way or another.

Spirit chooses to come and work with us, guide us, and point us in the right direction for all kinds of reasons and it appears it is always to improve this planet and the way we live in it.

Beautiful Planet

Visiting family or working with us is not the only reason Spirit pop into our world. With the beauty and the amazement of the Spirit world, I wonder why Spirit would choose to come to our world for leisure, to have a holiday or to visit this world. Yet if I look at this remarkable, beautiful planet of ours with my good eyes and not the pain, the greed, and the tortures of this world. I can see this planet as a wonderful abundant world. Much as I am left in amazement when I visit the Afterlife, I am also in equal amazement at the wonders of this world.

It is easy for Spirit to visit this world, for seconds, hours days or however long they choose, not forgetting there is no time in the Spirit world. The Spirit world is so close to ours, almost overlapping, that at the blink of a thought Spirit can be in our world.

I believe this is why many people see Spirits that have no connection to them in any way, or like me when I see random Spirits that don't in any way change my life. It's because they are not around for me, some Spirits really are here just having fun.

Many people who have visited interesting places will see Spirits in the holiday pictures or, at least, some kind of Spirit energy, again I think that's often random. We can be happily snapping shots and not even realise Spirit are also visiting the same place we are. We can go to an isolated place and feel the presence of Spirit yet somehow know they are not there for us. Again, these Spirits are also enjoying the same day trip we are.

Spirit children often pop into our world much like I pop into there's. Recently a woman told me she and her daughter had seen two Spirit children sat on the grass picking daisies. Before their eyes, the two children both disappeared. I had to laugh to myself as it reminded me of the times I was a child and I had gone into the Spirit world and sat on the grass picking daisies in their world. The two worlds are so connected that it is easy for Spirit to come and go as they choose.

When in Heaven, Spirit also has an endless list of things they do. Family gatherings, solitary walks, swimming, exploring the wonders of the Afterlife, meeting new people, and playing music, it's like one long free relaxing holiday. Sport is also played in the Spirit world.

Football Ahead

Pat was on holiday in Benidorm when she came to me for a reading, a middle-aged English woman with a nice dark suntan that combined well with her light blond hair. Pat gave me a friendly smile and sat down across my reading table.

"Your husband is in Spirit," I blurted out immediately. Pat nodded, and so the reading began, it was clear the Spirit of her husband Brian wanted to communicate with his wife.

Brian showed me he was pleased Pat had come on holiday to Benidorm. He told me she had almost cancelled the holiday and he was happy she did not.

Pat confirmed she had wanted to cancel the holiday as Brian had only died six weeks previous, but the family had insisted she continue with the holiday.

Brian had many messages for his dear wife Pat, including how he had liked the special flower arrangement at his funeral. He showed me a specific arrangement had been made for him, then he showed me single flowers, I was slightly confused with this, but I passed on the message as I was receiving it and Pat understood.

Brian told Pat she needed to continue living her life, although Brian's passing had been recent, he wanted to make it clear to his wife that she had a life to live, only one of them had died the day he took his last breath. Pat understood each message Brian was passing onto her. Brian also told me it was his mom who had come and picked him up and he had reunited with all the people he had loved and lost.

Then Brian showed me very clearly that he plays football with his Spirit friends on the Other side.

"Football?" I asked him aloud, although I wasn't surprised Spirit played football for some reason.

Brian confirmed to me that he plays football whenever he and his friends wanted to. Pat told me that Brian was a huge football fan and yes, he did have many friends who had passed and who played football. She also told me about the "special" flower arrangement she had made at the funeral. It was a football arrangement and the single flowers I mentioned were because she had given one single flower from that arrangement to each of her children after the funeral.

Brian also talked about his family and gave me other information, including a locket Pat was having made for him and a tattoo one of his children were having done. Brian had come through to me just as he had been in life, a fun, happy and caring person who loved his family and loved his football. It was nice to know he is now able to be by the side of his family who are alive whenever he wanted to and yet already had a fun and active Spirit life doing what makes him happy, playing football.

I believe the Spirit world has a huge amount of sports activities. Once while visiting the Spirit world, all my Spirit friends disappeared as they all rushed away telling me a basketball match was about to start. I was asked to join them, but I wasn't fond of sport even in the earthly world, so I declined from spending my time in the Spirit world watching sports. Another time I heard shouting in the distance. I had been sitting on the grass playing a game with a small group of friends. "It's a match," George told me. I didn't take too much notice but every now and again I could hear cheering from a distance.

Beautiful Garden

Once I found myself in a beautiful garden, it was almost like a large park. The grass had been cut perfectly, each blade the same as the next. There were flowerbeds and rockeries dotted around amongst several fruit trees. Everything appeared to glow, and I felt an overwhelming feeling of peace engulf me. I walked around the garden for some time. I realized I was alone and yet at the same time I was aware I was being watched.

The colours that surrounded me were incredible, perfectly set flowers lining up to create breath-taking patterns of colour. Shrubs and hedges had been cut with such straightness it was almost as if they had been cut with a knife.

Sculptures had been cut out of and trees to form enormous elephants, owls, horses, and other animals all perfectly cut, bringing art and nature together. I had never seen anything like it in my life.

As I stood in the amazing garden, staring at the works of art that had been created in nature. I noticed something twinkle from the corner of my eye. Twice something caught my attention but when I turned my head to look, nothing was there.

I walked over to where I had seen the twinkle, and again I saw nothing. Yet in the distance, I saw yet another similar twinkle, almost like a quick dazzling light. Again, I followed the light.

I came to a large, flowered archway, I passed underneath the arch tunnel and I was almost dazed by the magnificent smell of flowers as I walked beneath them. On leaving the archway I found myself in a different part of the garden, the grass was still cut perfectly, and the large sculptures created with hedges were dotted around, but now I could see many Spirit people were also there.

I was surprised at the contrast by going through the arch tunnel of flowers from the silence, to find so many Spirit people around me.

I walked forward and came across a man who was painting on a large canvas, I stood behind him and watched him paint, admiring his artwork.

He noticed my presence and turned towards me, he appeared to be a handsome middle-aged man with brown hair cut just below his ears.

"What are you doing here?" he asked me, surprised to see me.

"I don't know," I replied, wondering the same question.

I sat down on the grass and watched him paint, at first, it was exciting to see how he created such stunning art, but then I became a little bored with him and wanted to see what other people in the garden were doing. I walked around the garden for some time, and I realized everyone was painting.

Men and women from all ages were dotted around the garden painting, holding paintbrushes and canvases.

I noticed a small delightful looking pond. I headed towards the pond, and I saw a young black woman sitting by the edge of the pond, she wasn't painting, instead, she had a large drawing pad on her knees, and she was drawing a picture. I sat beside her and asked if I could have a look at her work.

She smiled at me and showed me the sketch she was working on. I couldn't believe it; she had drawn a perfect picture of me. I was astounded and I asked her how she could have drawn me when I had just met her now for the first time.

"I saw you when you walked into the garden a while ago," she told me.

I looked to where I had come from, "you couldn't have done," I said, realizing I was some way away from the flowered archway and there was no visibility from there onwards.

"In here," she said, raising her hand towards her head, indicating that she had somehow seen me in her mind. I was blown away and I spent the rest of my time in the garden talking to her and asking her questions as to what this place was. She explained to me that it was "Painter's Garden." A place where those who wanted to paint would feel inspired. She also told me that she had wanted to learn to paint and draw for a long time and now she was doing so.

I could have stayed there all day, and I think I did. It was like watching a film, I felt inspired just by looking around me and viewing the incredible colourful, perfectly sculptured garden. I was dazed as I watched Spirits painting while I was standing in such nature. I felt great to be in such a relatively busy place, compared to the countryside's and other nature spots I often find myself in, often alone or with just a few Spirits. Yet, it was a peaceful place, I could feel a calm creative energy surrounding me.

It was a kind of open art school for those who chose to spend some time painting and drawing and doing other artworks. It's definitely a place I want to be going to regularly when my time comes to pass over.

Learning Halls

The study halls of the Spirit world are open to everyone. Many times, when I have visited the Afterlife, I have stumbled across these vast halls.

The first time I went to the learning halls was when I was a very young girl and I was having a silly discussion with my Spirit friend George, I had told him something and he was insistent I was wrong. Being as stubborn as I am, I had to disagree with him, and we continued this conversation for some time. Finally, George told me to follow him.

We walked and talked for some time, and I didn't really take much notice as to where we were walking to or how far we had gone from our tree where we had started our adventure. We walked amongst some familiar countryside and took a turning through a small gate, as we passed the gate I noticed a tiny stream with a small bridge above it, we walked over the tiny bridge and came across even more countryside. In the distance, there were many large trees and we headed in the direction of the trees.

George was making me laugh the entire journey and before I knew it, we were standing by huge oak trees. What was behind the oak trees shocked me the first time I saw it.

I gasped in amazement as I saw what looked like a small town with huge buildings, there must have been around a hundred of these dazzling impressive buildings, they were all shining in a strange material that I have no words to describe, but they were all shining.

I was surprised to see what appeared like hundreds of Spirit people from all ages coming and going in and out of the various buildings. George lifted his finger to his mouth and indicated that I keep quiet, which I did.

I followed George as we headed over to a large building, as we walked inside it became apparent to me that we were in a large school, although it appeared friendlier and happier than any school I had seen in the physical world.

I'm not sure if George had made a mistake or if he had just wanted to give me a small tour of this building but we walked around this immense building for some time. I took note of everything and everyone I was seeing. Large halls, huge classrooms with classes taking place inside each room, just as in any earthly school. We came across a large room with only three young lads inside. George entered and said something to one of them, they all smiled at each other and chatted while I waited outside in the hallway looking inside. I noticed the classroom was full of books and the lads were making some kind of graph on a large board, similar to a chalkboard but extremely different in the sense it was shiny and silver.

George said goodbye to the lads, and we again walked around the large building until we arrived at the door where we had entered, people were hurrying past me by the door until George indicated that we continue outside. We walked past several of these large buildings, one of them stood out strikingly from the rest as it displayed a magnificent garden out the front. In the garden was thousands of plants and herbs and all sorts of greenery, it was a mass of smells, flowers, and shrubs. I noticed how people were standing around the plants with notebooks and pens, inspecting all the plants. It was as if they were studying the nature that was growing before them. Everyone appeared engrossed in what they were doing.

I followed George for quite some way, and I wondered where all these people had come from, the entire walk from our tree on the hill to this place, we hadn't seen a soul and yet there were so many people here I wondered how come I had never been before.

George indicated me to follow him as we approached a large, impressive building. "Shushhhh," he whispered to me as we entered the building, I was about to tell him I hadn't spoken but I was cut short as we walked into silence.

Never in my life had I heard such silence. We were in a library, the masses and masses of books struck me as incredible the moment I entered the building, but it was the feeling that everything was on mute that astounded me. I wondered for a while if I had gone deaf, as I honestly couldn't hear a single sound.

I followed George to what appeared at the time to be a sophisticated electronic object and today I would most likely call it a computer, George played around on it for a moment, touching his hand to the screen almost as if he was having his palm read by the screen. Then we were off again, I followed him around this massive library until it became apparent he was looking for something. He smiled as he looked at a number above a passageway, then he looked on a bookshelf that was stacked full of books and pulled out a smallish size book, he opened the book and found the page that he was looking for, and then he smiled again and shoved the book under my nose.

I couldn't believe what he was showing me, it was the answer to the silly discussion we had been having earlier. It now seemed like hours ago that we had talked about that subject. George smiled with a look that said, "I told you so." I burst into fits of laughter; I could not believe he had brought me all this way to prove his point. My laughter came out of my stomach and my mouth, but no noise came out of me, I was amazed that I was laughing in total silence.

I pointed to my open mouth, indicating to George that no noise was coming from me, he also began to laugh, and no noise left his mouth neither.

We laughed all the way out of the library, and it was only when we had left through the same doors we entered that our laughter was heard, I could hear again.

I have since returned to these study halls on several occasions although I only ever returned to that particular library on one more occasion and again, my visit was in pure silence.

I believe as Spirits we continued to learn, we don't die and know everything there is to know, we learn and evolve. I believe this study "town" is a place you can go to learn, you can go to visit for the day, or you can join a course, you can teach, and you can share. Much like the educational system in our world only far better as I believe we learn what we need and want to learn.

I also believe that this study place holds buildings where experiments are happening, experiments that will in some way be brought into our world, like cures and medicines, advancement in technology and arts. Everything that is in our world has first been created in the Spirit world by Spirits that have taken part in their development.

That doesn't take away any of the credit from its creator, but I believe Spirit are involved in helping the inventor invent, the creator create, even to bring the product into the world from just a thought to an actual thing.

If a medicine is invented in the Spirit world for our physical world, then they have to introduce it into our world somehow. They will find the correct candidate, more than likely someone who is looking for the same, say a doctor who is trying to discover this same medicine. He will be guided to find the right idea. From that point forward until it can be used on those who need it, many doors need to be opened, a lot of magic has to happen. I believe Spirit are involved in each part of the process. It's a highly evolved adventure and many people along with Spirits work and learn hard to bring about a better world.

CHAPTER 11

A Day in The Life

Over a lifetime of talking to Spirit and entering their world, I have been able to piece together a map of the Afterlife almost like a huge puzzle map, always aware that I have many pieces missing and much more to see. However, I have also been very fortunate to be able to live a day in the life of Spirit and see what it is they actually do the entire day.

George

I was laying on the sofa one sunny English day. The sun was shining through the window warming my skin, I felt relaxed as I enjoyed time for myself with a rare moment of an empty house. My children were young at the time, and I had a list of all the interesting things I was going to do while they were both with my mother for the day. What I hadn't expected was to not leave the sofa and yet have such a magical adventure that I can still recall as clear as if it happened yesterday.

Almost instantly, I found myself in the Afterlife. I appeared standing at the bottom of the hill with the large tree. Excited to find myself in my favourite place, I ran up the hill and found George. He was playing with a small group of young children. I had been visiting this same place since I was born. I had grown and aged, yet George still appeared to me as a 17-year-old lad. His dirty dark blond hair, and his long chin, along with his cheeky smile, always seemed permanent with him.

George was happy to see me and immediately we started to talk, he told me he was watching and playing with the children who were visiting. I knew he was taking good care of them just as he had of me when I was a child.

One of the children came running up to George and asked him if they could go swimming. George gave them a nod as he smiled at me and winked, "I'll take you through a shortcut," he said to them as the children jumped around in excitement with the thought of their upcoming adventure.

I rolled my eyes at George remembering well the shortcut that he had showed me many years previous. "Let's go," George shouted, and like the pipe piper, he walked ahead, and the five or six children followed him.

I walked along next to George, taking in the magic of the scenery surrounding me. I was so happy to be back in the Afterlife and now I was working as a medium I had a million questions for George, yet at the same time I felt so at peace, so relaxed I almost didn't want to talk.

As we reached the familiar lake, the children all started to jump into the water, swimming like fish. I sat down on the grass next to the lake admiring the view and remembering my own childhood times playing there.

George sat in front of me smiling. "What do you do all day?" I asked George with genuine interest.

"Lots," was his short reply.

Again, we became silent, I wanted to ask him what kind of "lots," and yet I no longer felt the need to know, I was too happy, too peaceful. I could hear the magical musical notes of the water, I could hear the beat of the trees, the sounds of nature were almost hypnotising me. I felt the heat of the Afterlife, the rays of love warming every part of me. I felt so at peace and so loved.

I was quickly brought out of the peaceful moment when George stood up and jumped into the water. The children all started to scream with delight as George splashed them and threw them around in the water. One of the young girls reminded me a lot of myself when I was a child. She had mousy brown hair that was shoulder length and straight. She laughed so much I could see colours jumping from her madly, she appeared like a disco ball on turbo. I looked at her and wondered if she was a Spirit child or if she had come for a visit as I myself had.

After the noise of the laughter and the screams of fun from the children, George jumped out of the lake and told the children it was now time for them to go. None of them wanted to leave and it took George some time to be able to get them out of the water. The little girl who looked a bit like myself came over to me and pointed at me. "Are you dead?" she asked me.

Shocked at her question I smiled and replied to her that, no I was not dead, at least I thought I wasn't. George laughed and told her to run along with the others.

Finally, the children were willing to return, and George told me he had to take the children back. We began the return walk to our hill. George was talking to me the entire way along the path and when we reached the bottom of the hill, I turned around and noticed all the children had disappeared.

"Where have they gone?" I asked George almost panicking.

"They have all gone home," he replied to me smiling.

I laughed as I remembered how easy it was to appear and disappear in the Spirit world.

George and I continued up the hill and as we reached the top of the small hill, I noticed another small group of five or six children who were happily waiting for George. They saw him and enthusiastically came running over to him and he greeted them all.

George set up a game for them under the tree and they played happily. On occasion, they came over to George to ask for help with the game or an answer to a question. George laughed and played with them.

I realised at this instant that this is what George does while in the Afterlife, he spends his days looking after children that have entered the Spirit world. George was a fun, caring and loving Spirit who had chosen to work with children.

After the second group of children also vanished, after pleading with George to stay a bit longer, George told me he was going for a walk, and we headed down the hill and along the pathway. After a few turns and twists along the way, we came across a warming country looking cottage. As we approached, a large woman with short grey curly hair came running out excitedly.

George ran up to her rather happily and they chatted for a while, the woman looked over at me and gave me a huge smile and waved, I smiled back. I immediately liked the woman and I felt like I would have liked to enter her cottage and spend the day with her.

However, after a short while, George said goodbye to the woman and walked back over to me. "That was my nan," he said to me.

"Don't you mean she is your nan?" I asked rather confused.

"No, it doesn't work like that, she was my nan," George replied to me. At the time, I did not understand this, but I know now that she had been his nan in his last lifetime, now she was a Spirit she was part of his Spirit family, but she was no longer his nan in the way she had been when alive. It was clear that she and George had a good relationship and a lot of love for each other.

"Do you visit her often?" I asked while at the same time taking in the beautiful surroundings I was seeing as we walked.

"All the time," George replied to me.

We then continued to walk along the pathway until we came to what looked like a busy village. There were houses and buildings spread around small narrow winding streets. A perfect picture village that looked almost unreal in its cleanness. George met with a group of men. I noticed that although they all shared similar colours beaming from them, one of the men was a short Asian looking man and another was a large built man with brown hair and a roundish face. George walked over to them, and they all looked at me, as they looked at me, they smiled and nodded as if to acknowledge me. I waited for George for a while and then I slowly wandered around the busy village.

It appeared such a friendly place and the many Spirits that were there were happily going along with their business. Although it was busy, it was also extremely peaceful.

Unfortunately, I had little time to explore the village as George caught up with me and indicated it was time to move on. We left the village and walked along the pathway back into the singing silence of nature and fields of many flowers. George told me that the larger man with the brown hair had been his brother who passed some years previous. It was clear George had admiration and love for his brother.

He explained to me that the shorter Asian man had a daughter who was still living and was very sick and that soon she would be joining them in Spirit. George was helping to arrange for Spirit children to visit the little girl while she was ill and to be with her during her dying process.

I ask George if he could do anything to save the girl and George shook his head from side to side. "Surely you can do something or talk to someone?" I asked him again.

Again, shook his head. "It's her time, she has to come home," he said to me with no sadness.

"She will be fine once she's over here, it's only while she's there she needs help," he said to me as he turned onto yet another pathway.

I continued to follow George around until we suddenly stopped at a large boat lake. Surrounding the lake were hundreds of Spirits. Surprised at the amount of noise and activity, I sat with George within the crowds of people as we watched a boat race.

George was really enjoying the excitement of the race although I was a little unsure of who I was cheering for, also as to who was actually winning. I found it incredible the way the boats would often disappear for brief moments causing the crowds to roar, it was a bit like the channel of the TV tuning out briefly when everyone was watching their favourite program. It was clear George was enjoying the race and there was a lot of cheering from him.

At one point George left me to go and speak to someone he knew and had seen in the crowd. I sat in the sea of colourful crowds, watching the boats in delight, and enjoying the atmosphere of the race.

A tall man with a mop of white hair and a large moustache was walking within the crowd. I noticed him and the vibrant mix of colours that were beaming from him as he approached me, he stopped directly in front of me, "should you be here?" he asked me in a friendly tone.

"I don't know," I replied to him honestly.

He smiled at me and continued to walk past me.

George returned and told me to follow him, which I did without question. After a while, we left the noise of the cheering of the boat lake. He took me to a small group of people who appeared to be having a small party where music was playing loudly. Although I couldn't find the source of the music, I did recognise the songs and I bopped around a little in an attempt to dance. I noticed quite a few people from the party had gathered around George on seeing him arrive and were talking to him intensely. I saw George nodding and smiling, and I realised that although he only looked like a young 17-year-old lad he was actually a very wise and sought-after soul.

I saw George come over to me, "I have to go, don't go anywhere, I'll be back for you," he said as he disappeared before my eyes. I wasn't too bothered I had been left in a stranger's party, in fact, I continued to bop around to the music, and I felt like I didn't have one problem in the world.

A tall woman came dancing over to me. "He's had to go," she said to me, pointing to where George had disappeared.

"Where's he gone?" I asked out of curiosity.

"To your world," she replied to me. She must have seen the look of surprise on my face because she then continued, "He has family who are still alive and he watches out for them, he's gone back to be by someone's side."

Before I knew it, George reappeared, and he immediately returned to a small group in the party. He spoke to them for a while until he finally came over to me and suggested we move on.

As we left the party, everyone waved us goodbye, and it was clear George was very well liked.

After the party, I followed George again along the path until I started to recognise where I was and soon, we had reached the small grassy hill with the large tree. As we walked up the hill, I noticed another small group of children waiting for George with excitement and George smiled as he greeted them.

He appeared to be happy to have encountered another group of children and they all ran to greet him.

"You better go," he said to me, and as I heard a young boy in the group ask George if they could play with the kite, I smiled as I remembered how much fun playing with the kite on the hill was. In that moment, I woke up on the sofa where I had started my journey.

It has become clear to me that George is actually a very active Spirit and not just with children, although it is evident George has chosen to work with children and he obviously loves it because he is always smiling and happy.

George appears to have a full life in the Spirit world, and he is constantly on the go. Not only does he help children but also, he creates friendships with them individually as he did with me. He also has time out where he can enjoy sports and parties and visit his Spirit family as he did with his "nan."

The journey I experienced with George that day was just a pebble in the pond of everything he actually does in Heaven.

It also brings home to me just how many children actually do visit the Spirit world and for whatever reason this is not only enjoyed by Spirits like George, but also encouraged. Although I have been asked many times the same question, "should you be here?" I have never been told I should not be there, nor have I ever felt unwelcome.

Paul Sows Seeds

Many years ago, I was living with my husband and children in the Spanish town of Blanes in the Costa Brava. One hot sunny day I had a reading for a woman named Angela. It was within minutes of Angela entering my reading room and sitting down on my old dining room chairs that I felt the presence of a Spirit man. Angela became excited as she confirmed that the Spirit man I was seeing was her uncle Paul.

Paul was a young, good-looking man who had been a soldier when he was alive. Paul told me that being a soldier had been all he had wanted to do when he was a child, and he was very proud to wear his uniform.

In very sad circumstances, it was while Paul was on leave from the army that he had a very unfortunate accident and died.

Although Paul gave messages of love for his niece and for his family it was the details he told me about his life in the Afterlife that has stayed with me all these years.

Paul told me that he was not only happy in the Spirit world but also that he was very busy. He explained to me in more detail than I normally receive when I give a reading, about what he does in Heaven. Paul told me that he continues to fight for the world, only in a very different way.

Paul explained to me that he now goes to all the important military meetings around the world. He told me he was very active in the army, helping in ways that were beyond my thought lines. He made it quite clear to me that he cannot just stop a war, he can't just bring world peace on the table and expect millions of people to pick it up.

He told me that he loves his life, although he is obviously no longer a foot soldier, he is actually helping the military more from where he is now than he did when he was alive. A large part of Paul's work in the Afterlife is to help the right people make the right choices, bringing about a better world.

Paul told me that his job was hard and there was a huge process in place involving many Spirits. I don't believe I will ever see world peace in my day, but I do feel that the little things that Paul is helping with now are like seeds, Spirits like Paul are somehow planting seeds for a brighter, distant future. How exactly Paul is helping I'm unsure, however, sometimes when I see world leaders on the television I wonder if Paul is one of the Spirits standing beside them trying to guide them to make the right decisions.

Paul explained to me that being present at meetings around the world with officials who held the future of countries in their hands was important to him and he spends most of his days in our world so as to be present at these meetings. Still, he told me that he also spends a great amount of time in the Afterlife doing what he loves. He told me clearly that in the Afterlife he studies, he plays, and he spends time with his family, both those living and those with him on the Other side.

Paul told me that he was a very busy Spirit and that he was enjoying his life to the fullest.

Angela asked me how he was able to do so much on the Other side and immediately Paul showed me that in the Afterlife the lack of time meant he was able to do everything he wanted to do. However, because he was often in our world attending a military meeting he also had to abide by our timetable. "If a meeting is a 12 o'clock, then at 12 o'clock your time I have to be there, I can't go early and I don't want to go late," Paul told me. He also explained that because he could be where he wanted in as quick as a thought, this meant he didn't need to wait around. Paul could happily be studying in the Afterlife and when it was time for the meeting in our world, within seconds he could be there.

Angela asked him, through me, if there was much point in what he was doing, standing around and listening to meetings with top military bosses from the globe, when he couldn't be seen or heard.

His input seemed rather limited. Paul told us that he couldn't be seen or heard, but he made sure his presence was felt, he explained to us that a large part of his mission was to try to make those involved feel compassion and justice.

I thought the information I was being told was rather wonderful, however, I did wonder if Angela could appreciate the reading, after all, I was used to telling people how their loved ones were by their side in Spirit and talk about fluffy puffs of energy in the magical land of singing water.

It turned out that Angela herself was also in the military and actually, she had a higher position then her uncle Paul had when he was alive. Not only did she understand the messages, but she also told me she wouldn't have expected anything less from her dear uncle who was faithful to his work when he was alive and clearly just as faithful on the Other side. Paul had made the military his life in both worlds, and he was happy he was able to sow his seeds for the future.

I personally didn't understand Paul's work in the Afterlife to help the military in our world. My rose coloured glassed could not get my head around men in uniforms with guns and power. I knew that in the Spirit world there were no wars, no military, and no separation. The Spirit world is a world without colour, religion, race, or borders. Every Spirit in the Afterlife lived in harmony, and I couldn't understand why a Spirit who lived in such a peaceful place would choose to come to our world to help with wars.

Yet Paul made it clear to me that if he could stop all wars around the world then he would. Unfortunately, our world wasn't so simple. We needed the military to help us survive attacks from others. Paul couldn't bring peace into one country and not in all. Doing so would leave that country open to all kinds of attacks. Paul's mission was a long one that involved Spirits from all over the physical globe. In the meantime, however sad it may seem, the military defence of each country is the only means of survival from enemies. Our soldiers are our only defence until we shadow the Spirit world and are war free.

I felt like this was one of the biggest differences between the two worlds, other than physical disabilities, that don't exist in the Spirit world. War was the biggest differing factor between the two worlds.

Vegan Florence

I met the Spirit of Florence many years ago when I gave a reading to a female family member of hers. Florence was a young exotic looking woman with what had appeared a happy future ahead of her. Florence was found dead in her home due to an unsolved murder. Neither Florence nor her family member talked much about her death, but Florence did talk about her life now she was in Spirit.

Florence showed me that she was enjoying a full life in the Spirit world, she showed me she enjoyed long walks in nature, she enjoyed time with her family who had passed over, and she was a very busy Spirit who did a lot of activities and including traveling our physical world.

Florence told me that she was now actively working to save animals. Florence explained to me that she had chosen to work with animals since her passing and although, when she was alive, she hadn't had a problem with eating God's creatures, she did spend her time in the Spirit world working to help create a meat free eating physical world.

Florence explained to me that she was part of a very large group of Spirits that were finding ways to spread the message across the earth that eating animals, or their products was cruel and unnecessary.

I wanted to stop Florence and her message and explain to her that we living need meat to survive. However, Florence jumped in before me and told me that eating animals was not only sad and painful on the animal, but it was also bad for the environment. Florence then continued with her vegan mission and told me that every time I ate an animal or part of it, I was actually mixing the suffering, the pain and the death of that animal's energy with my own energy.

I wondered in what way she was helping our world and as I thought it, Florence replied to my thoughts. She told me she spreads little thoughts around the world, "like magic dust," she said with a smile. Florence told me she switches the TV over when she wanted to try to get a certain person to watch a program that she thought would help them find compassion for animals. She told me she was able to "accidentally" get certain emails to go to people whom she thought would benefit from reading it. "And does that work?" I asked with interest, wondering if her little ploys to get the world to change by sending snippets of knowledge to people one by one could possibly work.

Florence told me it was not easy, but she was determined to empower people with knowledge as to the reality of animal cruelty in any way she found possible.

I was rather pleased when my reading with Florence had ended, and I was just glad my client explained to me that she had become a vegetarian two years previous and understood the messages better than I did.

For a few days after the reading, I couldn't stop thinking about what Florence had told me, the hard work she was doing while in the Spirit world appeared to be important to her and I felt somewhat guilty that I hadn't really wanted to listen. I had felt strongly that Florence was busy arranging meetings and giving inspiration, like little whispers in the ears of those who could make a difference to the lives of millions of animals.

I started to see the word vegetarian and vegan appear all around me and I realised that we were actually entering an era where it was no longer looked upon as strange to eat meat free. I read a few random emails I was sent by organisations that I wasn't a member of, and I knew somehow that it was Florence who was behind my newfound knowledge.

I stopped eating meat altogether and as an unexpected benefit, I began to feel and look better than I had in a long time. After the first few months, I had more energy than I had ever had. I was nourishing my body with healthy alternatives and enjoying new cooking adventures with different vegetables. I don't believe I have ever felt so good physically. Sadly, eight months later, I ignored Florence and her messages and enjoyed a large steak with pepper sauce, it was downhill from there, and I returned to eating meat.

This last year I have been investigating meat eating, or dead animal eating as it is and I often hear or read something that Florence told me over a decade ago, I think about her sometimes and wonder if she is the co-creator of the words I am reading or listening to.

I do know, though, that Florence is a powerful Spirit, and I am sure she, along with many other Spirits are still trying to convey the message to the world that animals have feelings, and are also energy, just as we are.

Carol Travels the World

Hospitals are bursting at the seams with Spirits. I believe this is because a lot of people in hospital are rather dying, in which case a Spirit loved one will be waiting to pick them up and take them over or it is because those who are sick are often feeling lonely, sad, or scared and Spirit are by their sides to somehow give them love and support.

Whatever the reason I see more Spirit at hospitals than almost anywhere else, children's schools and nurseries being equally full of Spirits due to the amount of Spirit family members that want to come close to children and watch them and gently guide them. More so when a child is away from its family, like when they are at school.

I also see many Spirits at care homes for the elderly. Interestingly the place I see the least Spirits is in cemeteries. This doesn't surprise me, when I die, I certainly won't be hanging around a cemetery either. I do, however, sometimes see Spirits that enter and leave a cemetery with a loved one who has gone to visit their graveside.

Not long ago I gave a reading for a woman named Elaine. Her sister Carol, who had died of cancer some years previous, came through to me during the reading. Carol was a fun, chatty Spirit and Elaine was almost squirming with delight with the messages from her sister.

Carol showed me that a good friend of hers was very ill and that she had been sitting with her in the hospital every day. Carol showed me that by sitting with her friend she was somehow able to transmit energy to her so she wouldn't feel so alone. Carol showed it to me as if it was like a wave of peace that she was able to pass onto her sick dying friend.

Carol gave me a small glimpse of her daily life, this included the preparation for her friends return to the Spirit world, the welcome home party.

Carol also showed me that she was a very busy Spirit, being able to travel the world with just a thought was a sure bonus for her as it appeared she was making the most of her time in Spirit and traveling around the earthly world. Carol told me she was going to visit every country in the world.

Elaine laughed hysterically when I repeated her sister's words and after her outburst, she told me that while Carol had been in the later stages of her illness, Elaine had asked her sister if there was anything, other than making her well again, that she could do for her.

"Anything you want, just tell me," Elaine had asked Carol very seriously.

"I want to travel," Carol had replied.

Rather surprised with the request and almost regretting starting the conversation Elaine asked her sister, "Where would you like to travel to?"

Carol looked intensely at Elaine and whispered, "Every place in the entire world." Elaine and Carol had both burst into fits of laughter. Elaine told me that Carol was unable to travel any further than home and then to her grave. However, Carol was showing me that actually, she was making her last wish come true and she showed me she was having the time of her life doing so.

Not only was Carol popping in to see her dying friend in the hospital every day, but she was also participating in the organizing of her friends return home party and in between thoughts she was traveling the world.

Yet carol showed me her life was even more interesting as she had also joined a choir and was involved with other group activities.

In between Carol's apparently busy days, she also spent time with her living family who were missing her, including her dear sister Elaine.

Elaine gained a lot from the reading, knowing Carol was enjoying her days in the Afterlife, however, I felt I also gained a lot from the reading as Carol had given me an insight into her life. Although time doesn't exist as we know it, it was pleasing to have it confirmed to me that however time is measured in the Spirit world it is used well. It was also good to see that when we become Spirits, we are able to travel anywhere we want with just a thought. Carol was using that ability to be able to move constantly between worlds, a trip to Rome along with a quick visit to the hospital to see a dying friend and then in the next thought she is able to be in the Spirit world singing in a choir with other Spirits. Carol was not only a busy Spirit she was also a very happy Spirit.

PART FOUR

HAPPY IN HEAVEN

CHAPTER 12

Our Beloved Pets

I have always loved animals and I have always had cats or dogs. My loyal friends have been by my side throughout all my life experiences. Giving me unconditional love, it's hard not to fall in love with animals.

It can be a devastating time when a loved one dies, the loss of our dear pets can also cause an equal amount of grief as the loss of a friend or family member, I have met hundreds of people over the years who have expressed to me their deep loss due to the death of a pet. Those who are not particular fond of pets often can't understand the pain others suffer when a four-legged friend dies.

The dying process is much the same for an animal as it is for humans, they live it much as we do and above all, they go to the same Spirit world we go.

Hundreds of animals have come through to me during readings and through the mind-to-mind international language of the Afterlife, animals have been able to show me they are still around their beloved owners, watching after them from the Other side.

Almost, Chula and the Doctor

When my small crossbreed of unknown prints got pregnant and had a litter of tiny pups the vet told us it was healthy for a bitch to have at least one litter. I had little money at the time, but I planned to give away the pups to good homes who would get a lifetime of pleasure from my offspring's.

Chula adored my husband Andres and was almost stuck to him, so it was no surprise when she had waited for him to come home before she went into labour, nor was it a surprise that he stayed awake all night with her, watching her and patting her and keeping all her needs met. Chula was happy her beloved Andres was with her and if my husband popped to the toilet she cried until his return. Finally, she brought her pups into the world. She was an excellent mother and we all fussed over her.

I had just finished a reading on a cold stormy night a few weeks after Chula had given birth. The thunderstorm had been loud, and Chula hated storms, so she had been anxious all day. When I left my reading room, I noticed Andres had started to panic. "This isn't because of the storm," he told me with a worried look on his face as he held Chula on his knees. "We have to take her to the vets," he informed me. Luckily, I knew the woman I was reading for, and she had not yet left, we had no car at the time, and she offered to take us to the vets in her car. It was night time and the sky had opened as it poured with rain but we had to get Chula to the emergency vet, however bad the weather.

In the car, Chula took a turn for the worse and Andres almost cried as she went stiff in his arms. "She's dead," I cried looking at her stiff lifeless body. "No, she's still breathing," Andres shouted back to me.

The sky was turning all shades of darkness, lighting up momentarily as the lightning struck. My dear client dropped us off at the emergency vet and we ran out into the rain without a single movement from Chula.

Andres hugged her as we rang the bell for the vet to open. After what appeared to be an eternity, finally, the vet inspected Chula. The vet informed us that Chula needed calcium or she wouldn't last the night. They sent an emergency car to the hospital to collect calcium. The thought of Chula not surviving was breaking my heart. How would our life ever be the same again if she wasn't at the door with her tail wagging to greet us, if she wasn't following Andres around the house? How could we sit and watch a film without feeling the heat of her lying between us as we stroked her soft silky fur?

For the first time, I truly understood those clients I had seen over the years who had showed such heartache when they had lost a pet.

Before the calcium arrived, the vet informed me of the many things that needed to be done to save Chula. "That's fine," I said not caring and just wanting my dog alive and well.

"It will cost around 2000 euros," the vet said to me as she did the math.

I wanted a hole to open up in the ground and eat me. I had not expected it to be so expensive. I couldn't believe it. How could I not save my dog? Chula had never in her life had a problem and other than check-ups and typical injections she had never needed a vet, so we had never paid the expensive pet care costs we had been told about. I wanted to kick myself.

"Do it anyway," I insisted to the vet.

"Are you sure you can afford it," the vet asked me very mysteriously.

"No, I can't afford it, but I can't let my dog die," I cried.

The vet wanted to know how she was going to be paid and I had no idea.

I stopped for a moment and took a deep breath.

"It will be ok," I said to my husband with confidence.

We heard the doorbell ring and the vet disappeared to open the door. Within the noise of the storm, I could hear the vet talking quietly. I could just hear her telling somebody that she didn't trust we had money to pay. Although I wasn't happy to hear her sharing my crisis with whoever had entered, her feelings were right, I didn't have money to pay.

The door opened and the vet appeared with a doctor from the hospital holding a bag of the lifesaving calcium.

I looked at the female doctor and I knew instantly Chula would live.

The doctor was a client of mine, I had given her several readings, and she had sent me clients for readings over the years. On seeing me the doctor turned to the vet and said, "Do what you must to save that dog, and don't worry about the bill," she turned and winked at me. The vet was taken aback, she was visibly shocked but immediately she went to work on my dying dog.

That was ten years ago, and Chula has never returned to a vet since. To think of not having Chula with us these last ten years is unthinkable. My readings that involved communication with animal Spirits were never the same again after that night I learnt a huge lesson from that thunderous night, and it brought me even more closely to understanding how heart-wrenching it can be losing a pet.

Blackie the Cross Lab

Doris came to me for a reading. Her husband had passed many years ago and he came through in the reading to pass on messages of love to his dear wife Doris. He was talkative and gave me quite a lot of messages, and although Doris was agreeing with everything I was saying, she appeared somewhat distant from the reading, almost uninterested in the messages from her departed husband.

"He's telling me he's with Blackie," I said. On saying these words, I saw an image in my mind of a big black dog. Interestingly I hadn't seen her husband, only felt his presence and heard him. Yet I did see Blackie the dog clearly.

As I told her that her husband was with Blackie, Doris suddenly became hysterical, she cried a bucket load of tears. At first, I was slightly confused, I assumed she must be upset because her husband had come through and she was having a delayed reaction to his Spirit presence. It soon became clear that the tears weren't for her beloved husband but instead they were for Blackie the dog.

Doris, within her tears, told me that Blackie had been the most important thing in the world to her. She told me that although she had loved her husband very much. Blackie had kept her company for the last 16 years of her life. Blackie had been the one who had been waiting faithfully at the door for her as she returned home to a lonely house. It was Blackie who had kept her company on what would have been lonely nights.

Blackie had shown Doris faithful love and he had also shown her how to live again. For the last 16 years, she had a reason to wake up in the morning, a reason to go for walks, to return home, and most importantly, she had a reason to live.

She had rescued Blackie two years after her husband had passed. She described those two years after her husband's passing as the worse years of her life. She had not really wanted the obligation of a pet, but Blackie had been abandoned and he was so tiny she felt an overwhelming urge to help him and take him home. She nursed him to health and Blackie grew and grew some more. He turned into quite a large crossbreed dog. Doris laughed as she explained she wasn't quite sure what he had been crossed with, but she knew he was born to be her dog.

It was the presence of Blackie that had brought her peace with the reading, not the messages from her husband. Although she said all the messages were appreciated, but the knowing that Blackie was still around brought her true joy.

Blackie showed me he was happy in the Spirit world, and he would often go and sit with Doris. Doris admitted she felt his presence often. Blackie also showed me he loved playing on the Other side, he had many other animals to play with and he no longer feared anything. Doris explained to me that Blackie had always been a fearful dog, hating men and loud noises or bangs. Doris had always assumed it was connected to the time he was abandoned. She was happy he no longer had that hurt and was playing with other animals.

Elli and Her Dogs

Maribel came to me for a reading in the middle of a Spanish heat wave, I had a small fan blowing in my room and I hoped I would be able to forget about the heat long enough to concentrate on my reading.

I had been reading for Maribel for only a few minutes when I noticed the Spirit of a young child come through to me in Spirit.

Elli was Maribel's daughter; she had died when she was just ten years of age. Elli had started to feel ill, she had a slight temperature, and as most ten-year-old children do when they get a bit under the weather, she went to bed. An hour later, she was dead, she had been sick and somehow had choked on her sick.

Maribel and her family were devastated by the loss of their sweet, happy Elli.

Elli showed me something rather odd. She showed me that shortly after she had passed over to the Spirit world, she got a dog. I thought it strange that she said she "got a dog." I then saw her with two small dogs, Maribel just smiled in silence to me, and I continued.

Elli showed me that her mother kept a very important white teddy of hers, it was a special teddy and Maribel confirmed that she did indeed keep a white teddy of Elli's and it was important because Elli had made it herself.

Elli then showed me that her mother also had an important necklace that she wasn't wearing on that particular day, yet she almost always wore it. Maribel told me that she always wore a necklace with a picture of Elli inside but due to the heat, she had removed it that day.

Elli then spoke to me about her brother Daniel, telling me that he didn't go to her funeral, but she was with him and by his side on such a hard day. Maribel confirmed this to me saying that she didn't allow Daniel to go to his sister's funeral because he was so devastated by his sister's death. Daniel was only 14 at the time and everyone, including himself, felt it best he didn't attend. Elli then showed me that he has since had a tattoo done for his sister, so she will always be close to his heart.

Maribel was emotional by now, she told me between tears that Daniel had a tattoo done of Elli, he had wanted it over his heart, but the tattooist had advised him to have it on his chest rather than directly on his heart. Daniel was proud of his tattoo, and it kept him close to his sister. It was clear Elli wanted her brother to know that she had seen the tattoo he had done for her, and she loved it.

Elli also showed me that she was with "Rebecca," watching over her. Her mother told me that Rebecca is Elli's cousin and they had been close. Elli then showed me that she was also with Pedro, watching over him, her mother confirmed Pedro was a school friend of hers who she had cared a lot about.

Elli returned to the beginning of her message and showed me again the importance of her getting a dog. Maribel then told me the story of the dog.

When alive Elli had been upset when Sally, their family dog had died, she had begged her mother for another dog, but Maribel was insistent that she didn't want any more animals at home. Finally, after lots of begging, Elli convinced her mother to get another dog. They arranged to view a litter of new-born pups and Elli fell in love with one of them. Maribel agreed that when the pup was ready to leave its mother, Elli would be allowed to take her home.

Elli had been excited the next few weeks while she waited for the day she could bring her pup home. The day they were supposed to pick up the new pup was the same day Elli had fallen ill and died later that evening.

A short while after the shock of her daughter's death, Maribel insisted on getting the pup and bringing it home, in a way she felt she had to get the pup in memory of her Elli.

Maribel and the family had another devastating blow when some time later the dog was poisoned and died.

It was important for Maribel to be told that Elli was with the dog and that she had witnessed how the family had picked him up and taken him home even after her passing.

Max the Dog

I was in the midst of what I thought was a good reading. Trudy, my client, had been listening intently to the messages her father had passed on to her through me and now I had begun communicating with her mother who was also in Spirit. Trudy was nodding in agreement with what I was telling her, until suddenly she interrupted me mid-sentence, "Is Max there?" she asked me. Taken aback I told her that I was only feeling the Spirit of her father and mother.

"Oh," she replied solemnly.

I gave a few more messages from her mother and again Trudy nodded in agreement.

"Your mum is telling me she's with your dog," I said. Trudy heard my words and started crying, it was the first emotional reaction she had given since the start of her reading.

"That's Max," she cried, "My Max." Trudy had a million questions for Max. She wanted to know if he was happy, who he was with and what it was like on the Other side.

I gave a full Spirit communication with Max, using the international Spirit language that all Spirits use. The messages from Trudy's parents were brushed to the side, maybe after the reading she was able to appreciate them more, but at this point, it was important for her to know her beloved Max, her best friend, was well and safe.

Trudy told me Max had been her life for a long time and she was devastated when somebody opened the gate to her home and Max had run into the street, directly into an oncoming car.

She screamed as she held his dying body in her arms and she had found no peace since.

The reading with her four-legged friend was what she had needed, and she told me she had actually asked Max to come through in the reading. For Trudy, knowing that Max came through with her mother made it even more important for her.

Trudy told me that the one Spirit she had been concerned about was Max. She knew her mother and father were together in the Spirit world; she knew that her mother was united with her grandmother along with other family members. What Trudy didn't know was who was with Max. Trudy fretted that because Max had nobody else in life other than Trudy, she wondered if Max was roaming around alone.

Max had shown me quite the opposite, he was happy and running in fields with friends of all species. He was with Trudy's parents, and he was with his own parents and his own siblings. Max was living a fulfilled happy Spirit life and he wanted Trudy to know it.

Maggie the Cat

When I told my client Anna that she had a cat with her in Spirit she actually stood up, walked closer to me, and gave me a kiss.

"That's all I wanted to know," she declared to me as she sat back down.

Although that wasn't actually all Anna had wanted to know, she then had a long list of questions for her cat Maggie, including if it was Maggie who sometimes jumped onto her bed.

Anna told me that since the passing of her dear Maggie, many a night she had felt something jump onto the bed and often she actually saw how the bed sank down slightly where the presence was. Anna told me that it was always on the side of the bed where Maggie had slept, and she was almost sure it was her.

Maggie the cat actually confirmed to me that she was the one who joined Anna late at night.

Anna felt much comfort knowing Maggie was still close to her. She told me how Maggie had been a large part of her life for 12 years, almost like a best friend. Anna had not thought she would be so grief-stricken by the loss of her cat, but it hit her hard. She asked me if Maggie was happy in the world of pets, and I explained to Anna that animals go to the same Spirit world we do.

"So, I can be with her again when I die?" Anna asked me rather excitedly.

I explained to Anna that when her time comes, no matter how long that may be, Maggie will be there waiting for her along with all those she had loved and lost. "Along with Skippy," I added.

Anna was surprised with my words, Skippy had been her first cat, she had only lived for four years and although Anna remembered her well, she had only been a child when Skippy had died and hadn't felt much loss. Anna was happy that Maggie and Skippy had met and that one day she would reunite with them both.

Buster

It's not only animals that keep watch on their owners when they have passed. Many Spirits have shown me they are still with their furry friends who they left behind in this world and that they watch over their pets from the Other side.

Andrew had died in his apartment; his dog Buster had been alone with Andrew's dead body for three days and nights before the police came. On arrival, the police found Andrew's dead body on the floor along with Buster who was lying next to Andrew's dead body. Although Buster had not eaten nor drank for three days, he still jumped up to faithfully protect Andrew when the police entered the apartment.

Jessica came to see me for a reading and her uncle Andrew came through with messages of love and to show her that he was fine and well in the Spirit world.

He told me to tell Jessica that he was grateful she had kept Buster and that she was looking after him well. Andrew told me that he often went to Buster and played with him and would often join Jessica and Buster when they went for their daily walks. It was clear that Andrew still loved and watched out for his beloved faithful Buster.

Jessica had no doubt that she would take on her uncle's dog. She knew how close Andrew and Buster had been and she had grown up with Buster in her life. However, she was happy that Andrew knew Buster was well and was now living with her. Jessica told me she knew her uncle would be keeping an eye on Buster.

All God's Creatures

It's not just our dogs, cats and other domesticated animals that enter the Spirit world upon death. All creatures great and small go to the same Spirit world we do when they die. They go through the same process with no difference. Dogs, pigs, chickens, birds, bees will play happily with cats, elephants, tigers, and bears. All animals have the same rights as we do in the Afterlife, and they all have happy and fulfilled lives.

I recently received a message from an animal rights organization telling me that animals are actually intelligent, pigs and chickens are more intelligent or as much so as our beloved dogs. I knew this already, for years while I had visited the Afterlife, I have fallen upon many Spirit animals, often playing for what seems like hours. Always being able to communicate with them in the same Spirit language I use to communicate with all Spirits.

I believe that all animals go to the same Heaven that we do, through the same process as we do and have a happy Afterlife just as we do.

CHAPTER 13

I Believe in Angels

What about Angels? If I refer to an Angel as a sexless flying being with wings as often portrayed in many films and books then I honestly don't know if Angels are real, not in that sense. However, if I consider Angels are highly evolved Spirits filled with the light and love of God then I do believe they are for real. Not only have I seen these beings on very rare occasion, but I have also heard about them by many Spirits.

It has been shown to me over the years that the Spirit world has a system in place, a fully functional system that keeps the entire Spirit world evolving and keeps it perfect. A system that we here on the earthly plane could learn a lot from and have the potential of following.

The Angel and the Kite

I remember once when visiting the Spirit world, I had been on the hill with the tree, playing with a kite. I was not alone, I was with several Spirit friends I had met over the years, some of them lived in the Spirit world, and some of them were visitors like myself. We would often ask George to bring out the kite and out of nowhere, he would produce the kite as we all jumped with excitement.

This one day we had all been looking upwards for what seemed like hours, watching our kite dance around. We all knew there was no wind, no breeze, maybe not even any air, yet the kite danced and played around us.

One of the girls in the group was only young, around six or seven. She was pretty with light blond curly hair and a small button nose. She danced as the kite floated past us. We hadn't seen her before, but we became friends with her immediately.

Although she was jumping around and appeared happy, we all noticed she had a very bad colour around her. She was a very dark murky brown colour that was somehow transmitting through her aura. It was disturbing at first, but my friends and I continued to play with her.

There was a point when we knew we all had to leave, it was a lot like the school bell at class time when everyone has to leave. We were about to leave when we heard the little Spirit girl say she wasn't going to return. I was surprised with her attitude and my friends and I decided to stay around and see what happens.

George was close by, and he came and told her in no circumstance that she could stay, she had to go back home.

"But I don't want to go home, I like it here, it hurts back there," she complained.

I wondered what she meant and immediately I understood that in the earthly world, this little girl was ill and suffering with pain, she had somehow gone to sleep and had come to play with us in her dreams.

George tried to consolidate her and convince her it was time to return but she flat out refused.

I knew George was having a hard time, so I approached her, and I tried talking to her, but she was a stubborn little thing and she refused to return. This went on for some time, with everyone in my group taking turns to convince her to return home. I knew that our time was up we should all be leaving.

Suddenly we all saw an amazing bright light appear, it wasn't a disturbing light, not like looking at a light bulb, but it was an incredible bright yet comfortable light. I heard George say, "Here we go," and shake his head slightly as he smiled, I wondered what he meant.

Just then, out of the light appeared a Spirit, but it was not a Spirit like the ones I had been accustomed to seeing, instead she was different. We all knew she was different. She was hovering in mid-air above us.

She had long golden hair and her eyes shone like the sun. Surrounding her little lights sparkled, almost like diamonds shining in the light. I had seen these diamond type lights many times in the Spirit world, but these appeared different as they were surrounding the woman.

Her voice was soft and gentle, almost like musical notes. She told the little girl to embrace her, and the little girl immediately ran into her arms. As the light had appeared, it disappeared, and both the woman and the child vanished before our eyes.

I was flabbergasted and after the commotion had died down, we all asked George what had happened. He had a cheeky grin on his face, and he asked us what we thought. None of us knew what had just happened but we all knew it was something special.

"She was an Angel," George told us. We had many questions about this beautiful woman, but it was our time to leave, and George refused to tell us any more about her.

I saw these special beings, Angels, on a few other occasions and over the year's Spirit have often spoken to me about them. Spirit has told me Angels are special.

Angels help both the living and the Spirits. Once, when I gave a reading to a client whose son had passed at just 33 years of age due to a work accident, my client asked me if her son had now become an Angel. Immediately her son in Spirit told me that no, he wasn't an Angel, but he did often go working voluntary for the earthly world and he met up with Angels. I somehow doubted him, like "What, you meet up with the Angels?" and he replied to me, "Yes, I have had the blessing of working in the presence of Angels," both his mother and me thought that was good enough and we were both impressed.

Angel Child

I had a wonderful experience while giving a reading to an English woman named Rose. As Rose sat down in front of me, prepared to listen to whatever may come out in her reading, I could see a small flashing light by her side. Amused and intrigued with the flashing light I couldn't help but stare. Within seconds, I saw the light grow into a large ball of dazzling light and within the light, I could see the Spirit of a child. I knew this child was an Angel, although I didn't see wings, I just knew, without doubt, she was an Angel.

I was told immediately who this child was, and I passed on the message to Rose as quick as I could talk.

"Your granddaughter who died before birth is with you, she is showing me she is an Angel, and she is by your side when you need her."

Rose smiled as at me, "She was stillborn," she replied to me.

"She's showing me she is an Angel by your side now," I said, hiding how excited I was myself.

"I knew, without doubt, she had become an Angel the moment I heard she had died inside the womb," Rose said to me.

The Angel child didn't stay for long and she didn't pass on

regular messages as Spirit do when they come to me to communicate. Instead, she wanted to tell her grandmother that it was true, that she was an Angel and that when Rose had felt her presence, it really was her.

"I have felt her with me so often since she passed," Rose told me. She then lifted up her sleeve and showed me her arm, she had a huge tattoo of an Angel child. "Look," she said as she showed me the tattoo.

"And look at this one," Rose said as she pulled down her top revealing to me a huge tattoo on her shoulder of an Angel child surrounded in a ball of light.

I had felt so much peace in the presence of the Angel child during the reading I gave to Rose and that feeling stayed with me for quite some time. It took me some days to stop smiling to myself as I realised, I had been briefly blessed by the encounter of an Angel.

Holding Hands

Susan was a Spirit mother who came through to me while I was giving a reading to both her daughter and her sister at the same time. Susan gave her family some interesting details of her life and snippets of private details that only her family knew. One piece of important information that Susan wanted to tell me was that she had met up with her Angel, Susan then showed me a wonderful image of herself holding hands with an Angel.

I was dreading telling this message to her family, "Hey, your mum says she's holding hands with an Angel." I was unsure if the message would be taken seriously but I passed on the message as it was shown to me. As I said the words both Susan's daughter and sister screamed with hysterics, leaving me wondering if it was screams of joy or sadness, apparently it was both.

Susan's daughter then explained to me that her mother had claimed to see an Angel many times throughout her lifetime. When Susan had taken ill, she told her family not to worry about her because her Angel would take care of her, and just before her passing, she told her family that she was going to be ok, that her Angel was going to come and "hold her hand."

Sweet Child

Another reading I gave was to a young Scottish woman named Jess, she had bright red hair and pale skin. She looked almost like she had just walked out of a Celtic storybook with her green eyes and brown freckles. She was stunning and yet I immediately felt an element of sadness around her. Minutes after starting her reading a young Spirit girl came through.

The Spirit girl was my client's daughter who had died only the year before. The daughter's name was India, and she was a sweet child who gave me some interesting messages for her mother. It was a very moving reading, which almost brought me to tears. The sweet little Spirit child talked in detail about certain friends she had and games her and her mum played when she was alive, she was showing me her memories, and it was very beautiful.

Almost as the reading was ending, India showed me that she was happy, and she was with the "Angel lady."

On saying those words my client smiled, her white teeth and her green eyes smiling out at me. She told me that when her little girl was dying, she had whispered to her, "Mummy the Angel lady has come for me," and within minutes, she breathed her last breath.

It was comforting for Jess to know that her daughter really had seen an angel before she passed and that she was now in the Spirit world happily coming through to confirm it to her mother.

Old man

It was an English man named John who died in his 80s that explained Angels to me slightly better. He had come through in a reading to communicate and pass on a message to his granddaughter who I was giving a reading for at the time.

John told me that in life he had not believed in the Afterlife or in Spirit. He then told me when he died, he was united with all of his relatives who had passed before him. He explained to me that he had been extremely busy since his passing, and he told me the following story.

Apparently, he had offered to help with a world problem. A global disaster that was of utmost importance and that apparently, he had the skills and the knowledge to be able to help on some level. On arrival to where he was to help, he met up with many Spirits like himself, all with different skills, and all with different knowledge. It was a gathering of souls with a mission in mind. He told me that due to the importance of the issue they had the help of Angels. Angels had intervened with a worldwide matter.

I asked him how the situation had ended, and he smiled at me and replied, "Well, you're still alive aren't you?" I took that to mean Spirit and the Angels accomplished their mission.

I have no idea what it was that Spirit and the Angels gathered to do on that important day, but it did make me realize just how hard Spirit work to help us with our everyday lives and with the planet. Also, when they need that extra help, it seems Angels are called upon.

I asked John a little more about Angels. John explained to me that Angels share the same Spirit world we all do. He also explained to me that they are wiser, more loving, and more evolved than say, Uncle Jim who passed last year.

I have often asked my own guide Micheal about the presence of Angels and the role they play in the Afterlife. Micheal has always explained it to me in a way that made me feel that Angels are those that help keep the system in place. Almost as if they are more part of the source than we are. I always feel that there is a huge amount of respect and love when Micheal has ever spoken to me regarding Angels and I feel that somehow, although they live in the same world he does, Angels have a more mysterious life in the Spirit world.

I know people who claim to have seen Angels with wings I also know of people who know the names of Angels and what each Angel are summoned upon for, like Michael in a moment of need and Uriel for healing and so forth. Although this sounds appealing to me, I have yet to come across these incredible winged beings and I have yet to be informed of Angels by their well-known names.

Wings or no wings, names, or no names one thing I am very certain of, is that in an almost non-traditional way, I do believe in Angels.

CHAPTER 14

The Sign Language

Of Spirit

To be able to communicate with the Spirit world we need to learn the language. I call this language, the sign language of Spirit. This language cannot be found in any translation book because it is unique to each individual. I have also found that there are no set rules when it comes to what signs actually mean what. However, there are a whole set of universal signs that people seem to understand around the world. Spirit will often use the same signs including feathers, butterflies, robins, and lights flickering, although the list is endless.

As it is an individual language Spirit will also use personal signs. My dad's song playing on the radio will mean nothing to anyone other than myself, or those who also have that same important song that connects them to someone they have loved and lost to the Spirit world.

Lucy and Her Pin

Lucy had a pin, every time Lucy saw a safety pin, she knew her grandmother was with her in Spirit, sending a sign of her presence. I asked Lucy why a safety pin was her chosen sign and she told me her grandmother never left the house without a safety pin, it was of somewhat importance to her grandmother.

On the day of her grandmother's funeral, everyone who attended wore a safety pin. What was amazing was the amount of pins Lucy and her mother had seen over the years. Safety pins would turn up everywhere for them, on the floor ahead of them, on the seat on the train. Lucy told me she even found one on her bed once and she knew it had not been there when she had left the room. Safety pins have followed Lucy around for the last four years since her grandmother's death and this strange habit of her grandmothers has now become one of Lucy's greatest signs that her grandmother is still with her.

The importance of the sign language Spirit sends us is to recognize the sign. It's only when you feel it is a sign and it stirs emotions inside of you that it is really a sign from a loved one.

I can't think of a time I ever found a safety pin; I can't ever remember seeing one in the street or finding one on the train seat or on my bed. This is because a safety pin is of no importance to me at all. Maybe over the years, I have stepped over a million safety pins, and I made no note of it all, my mind would have no reason to stop, look, and listen.

Yet I take the traffic light code with other things, like signs that to Lucy may seem unimportant or meaningless. Now a feather to me is an important Spirit sign, to Lucy it may simply be a passing bird has shed a feather, Lucy may take no notice from the feather of a passing bird, while I will find a huge amount of comfort in that same feather.

The difference is a knowing, it's an understanding of the language your loved one is sending you. It's a feeling within, that when you see a sign, a safety pin, a feather, a rainbow. It's when something inside stirs you and you accept it as a sign, even being open to the idea of something being a sign is because you understand it as so, you understand the language.

Although Spirit will send different people different signs, there seems to be a common link with certain signs. These signs are of great comfort to many people. To others it means nothing. The sign language of Spirit is all about feeling and connection. If you feel it, if you see something and wonder if it is a sign from your loved one, then it probably was.

Can Spirit really send us an animal, a bird, or a dog? Can they change the weather, bring out rainbows and make it rain? Can Spirit really play around with our electrical goods, turn our TVs off and move objects around? I honestly believe they can. I believe Spirit are capable of so much more than they are often given credit for. They work hard to make sure that one special song comes on just as you walk into a shop. They plan it so that car in front of yours with the license plate that says Joe, really is your uncle Joe saying hi. Spirit has the ability to work with our environment in such a way that we can see the signs and feel the language.

Here are some common signs, many may recognize the signs as the very same language Spirit use to talk to them, and others may feel no connection with these signs at all. The list of signs that Spirit send to us is individual and endless. I'm just starting with the very basis of a language that has no dictionary or rules and is very different for everyone.

Feathers from Heaven

Since the Spirit of Patrick came into my reading room several years ago, I have had an endless number of people talk to me about feathers they have received as signs from Spirit. I have also had Spirit talk to me regarding feathers regularly.

I spoke about Patrick in my first book Always by Your Side. Patrick had communicated with me to give a message to his wife, who I was giving a reading for. He came through loud and clear with many messages. One message that he told me was to tell his wife he would be sending her feathers. I was rather sceptical of the message, but I passed on the message as Patrick had asked. I was amazed shortly after the reading how not only was his wife, Ines, now receiving feathers from strange and random places, but I myself started to find feathers and have them come to me in strange ways.

I believe Patrick opened some kind of link for me, almost as if he had given me a new word, a new sentence. I started to receive messages from Spirit about them sending their loved ones a feather, something that I had never experienced previously. I would often find myself telling a client a repeated message as to look out for the feathers. Although in reality there is no need to look for a sign, the sign actually finds us.

Recently I asked Spirit about this feather phenomenon and how could it be possible. Spirit explained to me that a feather is so easy for them to move, as it's literally as light as a feather and Spirit can easily move the energy around it to move it to any place they choose. I wondered why Spirit had never showed me this before, but I was told by Spirit that they had done many times, but apparently, it had been too simple for me to understand at the time!

Robert was a classic example of this feather phenomenon that had now started to follow me around.

It was another hot sunny day and Benidorm beach was busy as the sun was shining at its finest. I was talking to a work friend in the shop where I worked as a medium and tarot reader. An elderly English couple came in. They looked around and then bought candles and an Angel. As they paid, I noticed all the candles they had bought had been decorated with crosses. The woman must have noticed me looking at the candles and she whispered over to me, "They're for my son's grave."

I had gathered they were for a grave, but I politely said how sorry I was for their loss.

Her husband appeared by her side, a tall elderly man, he turned to me and told me his son had died not long ago. "He went to work and did a double shift on the Friday, and he was dead by the Monday," he told me very solemnly.

I could feel their pain but again I was only able to reply how sorry I was for their loss. I saw a tear roll down the woman's face as she told me that Robert was their only son, they had other daughters but no more sons.

"He had died due to heart failure, just like that," she said as she clicked her fingers in a sign that told me it was a sudden passing.

"You know it's really lovely to buy these candles for his grave, but you do know he isn't there don't you?" I asked.

"No, I don't," replied the woman. She told me she had no idea where her only son was now, she wanted to believe that he was in another place, but she really didn't know for sure. She explained she felt close to him at his grave. I could understand what she was saying, and I could feel her pain in her words.

I lightly told her how I knew there was life after death. How I had seen Spirits all my life and how I had the most amazing experiences while communicating with Spirit. It was very unusual for me to talk about myself to customers in the shop. Although I worked there, normally I always waited for people to find me, always waiting for people to ask me questions rather than me intrude on their space.

However, this conversation felt different, I explained to the grieving couple briefly about the Afterlife, I noticed how they had both come closer to me and were listening to me with some kind of hope that what I was saying was true. Just then, I remembered Patrick. Right there in the middle of the shop, talking to an English couple about their living nightmare, I was suddenly thinking about Patrick. Was I thinking about him or was I feeling him? The couple had now paid for their candles, and I knew they would be gone soon but I had a desperate urge to talk to them more. Suddenly the words came flowing out of me.

"Why don't you ask for a sign?" I suggested, "I know due to previous and recent experiences that for whatever the reason there are certain signs that are easiest for Spirit to send."

I saw the couple look at me, but I was unsure what their thoughts were. I continued, "Ask your son if he is still around you to send you a feather, not just any old bird flying by that drops a feather, but a specific feather or a feather in an unusual place or in an unusual way." They both looked at me, thanked me and smiled, and then they left the shop.

As they left, I wondered if they would ask their son for the sign or if they had thought I was maybe a crazy woman. I did spend some time wondering why I had suddenly thought about Patrick and why I had suggested the feather. However, I smiled to myself. I knew by now to trust what I felt.

The next day I was in my reading room in the shop, another bright hot sunny Spanish day. I heard people in the shop asking for the "lady who said spiritual things." Slightly amused, I left my room and went into the main shop to see who was there and I saw it was the elderly couple from yesterday. Yet there was something oddly different about them both. On seeing me, they both came rushing up to me and I felt a burst of excitement as they told me their story.

After talking with me the previous day they had discussed what I had said, and they thought it wouldn't harm to try my suggestion of asking for a sign. The lady told me with all her heart she asked her son "Rob, if you're around, if you still exist, please send me a feather, an unusual feather or in an unusual place." She explained how she had asked with all her heart.

Later that day they returned to their hotel, and they sat outside on the sun terrace. They were chatting with their daughter who had come to Spain with them. As the couple were chatting the daughter suddenly asked, "mum what's that?" and as the lady looked down, she saw on her chest was a single white feather with a brown trim. She couldn't believe a feather had somehow appeared on her chest. Her husband told me he had been sat in front of her the entire time and yet he hadn't noticed the feather, clearly visible on her chest.

They then introduced themselves to me as Janet and Hayden, they thanked me so much for my suggestion, and they both explained to me how important that single feather had been. They had a knowing stronger than they had ever had since Rob's sudden death, that he was still with them, he still existed. It didn't surprise me when Hayden and Janet told me they were having a portrait of Rob made and they intended to add the feather they had received inside the frame.

The pain of losing their son can never be removed, not with all the feathers in the world. However, I knew they were a step closer to finding peace with his death. Knowing he was with them meant there was no death as such, it also proved to them that if life after death is real then one day when the time comes, they will again meet up with their beloved Rob. In the meantime, they still had a life to continue living.

Since meeting the Spirit of Patrick, I have become the feather woman in a way, having heard the same Spirit message repeatedly and had many clients return to me to tell me of their exceptional feather findings, each experience being unique and exceptional.

One lady, I did a reading for I gave a similar message from her husband about a feather, she seemed very sceptical at the time, but I felt calm knowing if Spirit were giving me this message there was a reason behind it. "I see lots of feathers," she told me very seriously when I passed on her message. I assured her that the feather she was about to see would be different, it would have something special and magical about it.

A week later, she returned to me to share her story. Apparently, she had decided to go to the big church in the old town of Benidorm. A place she often visited with her husband when he was alive, she told me during the entire walk to the church every few minutes she passed a small white feather on the path before her, at first, she just put it down to what it was, a feather, two feathers, three feathers and so on. She remembered the message she had received through me from her beloved husband yet at the same time, she brushed it off as just feathers in her path.

On entering the large church, she was quite happy to find some shade and get out of the heat of the blazing sun, she found a place to sit and walked over to sit down, only to find a feather in the place she was about to sit down. At that moment she realized something magical was happening, she wondered how a feather had fallen onto her seat in an enclosed church.

She sat down and began to talk quietly to her husband. she closed her eyes briefly as she started to feel her first moment of peace since his death. What if the feathers were really from her husband, she pondered to herself. She slowly opened her eyes only to find a large white feather falling before her. She caught the feather and realized that this was too much of a coincidence to be brushed off. The well-kept church had no roof openings and there were no birds above her. Again, she gained a feeling of peace from the feathers of the day. She started to see it as the magical moment it was.

Recently I gave a reading to a lady and her relative came through in Spirit, he showed me clearly that he was trying to send signs to my client to prove his presence, and more so while she was here in Benidorm. Almost as if he was proving to her that he had come on holiday with her. "He's showing me a feather, he's showing me he's sending you a feather and you will know it is him." My client smiled as she reached into her bra and pulled out a white feather. She explained to me that on that very morning, she had found a white feather and somehow, she had just known it was him. She felt as if he was telling her that he was with her in Benidorm. My message only confirmed what she herself had already felt.

I was hearing from people on a regular basis about the power of feathers, in a way I was intrigued and at the same time, I was beginning to become amazed myself with the magic of the feathers from Heaven.

Will was another classic example of the power of signs. When I first gave a reading to Will, his mother, and his ex-husband Frank, came through in Spirit. Will is a tall, slim Irish man in his 60s with a mop of grey hair. Will had a terrible early life and his life story could fill the pages of any book. Being homeless and searching for the bare essentials of survival had been part of his struggle of life since infancy. Will worked hard from below legal working age so he and his mother could live. Moving homes, jobs and the hunt for survival was continual daily life for Will.

When Will turned into a man he met Frank, the love of his life. Frank moved in with Will and his mother and due to hard work, they were able to find better times. They bought a house and lived almost happily ever after for many years.

Will's mother loved Frank a lot and the three of them lived well. When Will's mother took ill, Frank and Will both looked after her for years. She was treated like a queen and nursed by both of them until her death.

The passing of mother had been hard for both men and some time after her death, they took a holiday to Australia. It was when they were on holiday Frank became ill. They took a flight home and Will became a nurse yet again as he watched the love of his life die from cancer.

When I met Will, he was a lonely man. His entire life had

revolved around his mother and Frank. He was now lost without them both. His time was spent between lonesome holidays.

During our first reading both his mother and Frank spoke loud and clear, giving Will much comfort. Frank told him he was sending him signs all the time to say that he was with him still, that he still loved him, and he wanted Will to enjoy the rest of his life without him.

Frank then showed me a feather, he told me to tell Will to watch out for the feathers. I repeated the message to Will, and he told me he had already been finding strange feathers that had appeared.

I liked Will instantly and I soon started a friendship with him, and shortly after I introduced him to my mother. Since then, the three of us have become like best friends. I have laughed so much with Will that my stomach has hurt. I have heard every story he has to tell, since his birth, and we have shared all our worries and problems together, always ending in laughter. He has become a part of the family now.

Will did receive more feathers from Frank. In fact, Will received so many feathers he could make a quilt with them all. Feathers follow him around everywhere and more so tiny little ones.

Just before Will is about to come over to Spain, I always find a small white feather on that same day. A little sign for me from Frank to tell me to look out for him.

If you find a feather suddenly wondering towards you, or in unusual surroundings, maybe it's Spirit confirming they are with you and to let you know they are by your side.

Birds

I have countless stories from people that feel birds are a sign from their Spirit loved ones.

The first Christmas without his beloved Frank, Will returned to Spain for a holiday and returned to the same restaurant he and Frank had enjoyed their Christmas dinner the year before his passing. Lonely and feeling down, Will sat outside on the large sunny terrace, and sat at the table directly in front of the one they had sat at for the last Christmas together. Halfway through the meal, a bird appeared and flew to the seat Frank had sat on the previous year. The bird just perched itself on the back of the seat and stared at Will for a long time. In that instant, Will knew it was a sign from Frank. Not that the bird itself was Frank, but Will knew that Frank had sent the bird to show he was still with him.

Was this really a sign or was it wishful thinking from Will? After all, Will was sad and lonely, desperately looking for a sign.

I believe it was a sign from Frank, without a doubt.

For one, I believe that if it feels like a sign then it most probably is, that's the understanding of sign language, to feel it, but I also knew because of the first reading I had given to Will.

Not only had Frank come through in Spirit and spoke to me loud and clear. Frank then told me that the first Christmas after his passing had been very hard for Will. He told me that he had sent Will a sign.

"Did you see a bird staring at you on Christmas day?" I asked

Will during the reading. Will smiled at me and told me how he had known that bird had been a sign from his dear Frank.

Birds seem to be a sign for many people.

A woman named Mari who came to me for a reading recently told me that she had stopped to listen to a crow that appeared to be talking. "This crow was making the strangest noises," she told me. For some reason, she felt she had to stop. She listened to this crow making strange sounds and staring at her while turning its head from side to side, almost like it was in a full-blown conversation with her.

Mari told me that this continued for a good 5 to 10 minutes, she said she felt like a bit of a Loony standing in the street listening to a crow.

By the side of her, another woman stopped to listen to the crow. As the woman stood next to Mari, the crow went silent.

"I don't believe it," Mari told the woman, "That thing has been making a right noise."

"I know, I heard it while I was walking up the street," the woman replied.

The woman's name was Melissa, and the two women instantly began a conversation. This conversation led to a close friendship. Both women who were very much alone in life, one through divorce and the other a widow, had now found a friend in each other, to go to church with, to have coffee with and to share parts of life with.

Mari swears the bird was a sign from Spirit so the meeting between these two women could take place and they could start the important friendship they now have.

Butterfly's and Dragonflies

My special sign from Spirit for many years has been the butterfly or the dragonfly, both brings a message from Spirit close to me.

Years ago, when my close friend Dee died, I was devastated. She was not only my friend, she was the mother of two of my other closest friends, and she was also my spiritual support, guiding me with all sorts of issues I was experiencing as a budding medium.

Before Dee's passing, she had started a web page of a spiritual nature, a web place I was able to learn and grow. On this web page, we had all named Dee the butterfly, or the dragonfly, depending on our need at the time. I would ask questions on the webpage of issues that were bothering me at the time and when I saw a butterfly, I would excitedly run to my computer knowing an important reply had been left for me.

Dee had been writing a thread that lasted for three days, I hadn't understood the thread at the time. On writing the last thread, Dee had a massive heart attack and died three days later in hospital.

Since her passing I feel she has continued to guide me as she did in life, she has continued to share her spiritual knowledge with me and help me to become the medium I am today. Whenever I see a butterfly, I know it as a sign from my dear friend.

Butterflies represent many things to many people. From rebirth to the transition, from life and death. From the cocoon to the caterpillar, to the flight and the freedom that is the final process before the passing of this world.

However, for many people when they see a butterfly, they instantly remember a loved one who has passed. Many times, when I have given a reading, I will often hear myself saying, "Your loved one is showing me a butterfly." instantly the message is understood. Often my client will reply to me saying, "Yes, that's the sign they always send me," or something along those lines.

I told a similar message to Cathy, telling her that her son, who had passed over into Spirit and was now talking to me, was showing me butterflies. "He wants you to know the butterflies were from him," I told Cathy.

Cathy cried as she told me that some years previous, she had lost her son due to illness. He had been ill for a while and on a cold November night, he passed over to the Spirit world. He was only in his early 20s and Cathy explained to me how she had been left with a feeling of rage.

"One day I had watched a film about a dragonfly, and I asked my son that if he was ok on the Other side to show me a sign." Cathy continued to tell me her story.

"I told him to send me butterflies because I thought a butterfly would be a decent sign."

Cathy told me that nothing happened for days, and she felt the rage built up in her even more as she realized that her son wasn't around.

It was almost a week later when Cathy was driving home from

the supermarket. She had taken a shortcut home along a country road when her car broke down.

Cathy pulled her car over to the side of the road and not knowing much about cars she phoned a friend to come and pick her shopping up so it wouldn't melt until the breakdown van arrived.

As Cathy waited for her friend, she sat on the grass next to her car, it was a warm day and the sun had started to shine. She looked around her and realized how beautiful it was where she was sitting, since her son's death she had no interest in the beauty of nature at all.

As she sat on the grass she relaxed. It was the first time in a long time she actually felt for one moment, a moment of peace, she closed her eyes and let the sun warm her skin.

Cathy then told me the amazing thing that happened to her that day and changed her life.

She felt something on her face, brushing it off with her hand she opened her eyes, only to find herself surrounded by hundreds of yellow butterflies. Cathy was astounded as she looked at the many butterflies that had crept up to her within minutes, as her tears fell, she knew it was her son sending her sign. Cathy was equally amazed at how the butterflies appeared to only be surrounding her.

She said, "I looked ahead of me, and I couldn't see one, I looked behind me and not one and yet around me were hundreds of them."

In that instant Cathy felt the peace she had needed; she had recognized the sign from her son very clearly. It had taken a few days but her son to leave an impact had beautifully orchestrated it.

To add to Cathy's amazement, when her friend arrived to pick up her shopping, she had brought her little niece with her. Her niece was on her way to a fancy-dress party and was dressed as a butterfly.

Cathy has seen endless butterflies since that day, and she believes each time it is a message from her son. She also told me that even our meeting had been a sign from her son.

Cathy had not wanted to see a medium, she didn't want to open herself up to disappointment or someone taking advantage of her loss. Yet she had stumbled across me and had an overwhelming urge to see me.

When Cathy saw me, she knew the meeting was because her son wanted her to see me. That morning I had borrowed a top from my mother as it was a hot day, and I was overdressed. "I want it back," my mum said hopefully, as she passed me a T-shirt with a large butterfly on the front. I had also just found some large decorative butterflies in the shop and had placed them behind my chair in my reading room. Also, that day I had decided to wear my butterfly necklace and bracelet that I hadn't worn for a while.

Cathy had lovely communication from her son during her reading with me and although his confirmation that he was the one who sent her the butterflies was lovely, it was a message that Cathy didn't really need, she already knew it without doubt.

Rainbow and Other Weather Signs

Many people take changes in the weather as signs from Spirit. Like Wendy, a client of mine who I gave a reading to last year, during her reading her mother who had passed over into Spirit came through with messages for her daughter Wendy. One of the messages I was seeing was a rainbow, nothing else just a rainbow but I felt the rainbow was important.

"I'm being shown the importance of a rainbow," I said to Wendy.

Wendy smiled at me and told me that the moment her mother died in the hospital, a huge rainbow appeared outside the window of her mother's room. Wendy told me since then rainbows are her sign from her mother.

Another client I gave a reading for had a similar message from her mother who had also passed. This message was slightly more specific, "your mother is showing me that you were sat by the window crying and asking her for a sign to indicate that she had reached the Other side safely and in that instance a rainbow appeared."

My client let out what sounded like a small scream as she confirmed to me that this is exactly what happened. She was happy that it wasn't a coincidence and the rainbow really had been what she had thought it was, a sign from her mother.

I have known people who use other weather events as signs from loved ones also. A Spanish woman told me some years ago the sign that she gets from her husband is snow. She sees snow and knows it's her husband sending her a sign. She told me about a time they had gone on holiday together to England and it had snowed on arrival. Apparently, the snow had lasted for days. She told me that this unexpected snowfall had actually made it the best holiday they had ever had and sadly, it was their last holiday as shortly after their return her husband died from a massive heart attack.

"How on earth do you see signs of snow in Spain?" I wondered aloud.

"Oh, when my husband wants to send me a message, believe me, I see snow." She then told me of all the ways she sees snow when her husband sends his sign. She has received cards of snow images. She had clocked onto her Internet only to find a picture of snow, even in the summer. Friends from abroad had shared pictures with her of themselves in the snow and an endless list of events that as a single thing means nothing more than the fact it snows in the world.

Yet to her, it was direct messages from her husband. To her these snow signs not only helped her but also guided her. My client filled with tears as she told me what happened to her several years ago. She had been ready to buy an apartment from plans, although building work on the apartment had not yet started, she still felt the offer was exactly what she had been looking for. Buying an apartment on her own was a big step for my client but she was sure it was the way forward. The week before she was to part with her money, she saw many images of snow. In strange ways, snow was following her around in the form of images and words. Even a book she had been reading had now included a snow scene that reflected that last holiday in England she had shared with her husband.

At first, she assumed that the messages were her husband's way of saying he was with her as she took such a large step alone, but as the signs became stronger and clearer, she finally stopped and thought about it.

My client took some time out and went to sit on the beach and cleared her mind, she closed her eyes and whispered quietly to her husband, "If you are showing me the signs because I shouldn't buy this apartment then send me a clear image of snow. If it's because you are with me then send me something different, send me the sunshine, a clear image of sunshine."

After she had said these words, she felt confident that she would see a strong sign from her husband.

When my client arrived home, she found that someone had left her a magazine on her doorstep. She picked up the magazine and gasped in amazement. Staring out from the front page of the glossy magazine was a large picture of snowy England.

My client listened to the language of her husband, and she did not buy the apartment. Sadly, other people did, and they have all lost their money and are in long court battles. The construction company declared themselves bankrupt, the apartments continue to be pretty lines on blueprints, and so far, no one has had their money back.

Even after we recognize a sign for a sign from Spirit it's not always easy to understand who the sign is from or even what it actually means. My client had first thought the signs of snow were her husband's way of guiding her towards the apartment. It was only on further investigation that she realized something was wrong.

When I asked her why she had felt something was wrong, what had made her think her husband was actually showing her to steer away instead of buying? She told me because she thought about the kind of man her husband was. "He wasn't the kind of man to push me forward in anything, yet he was very protective of me," she told me. That is what had made her stop and ask him. She told me she knew he loved to send her signs to cheer her up and to show her he was around but an unusually amount of signs was unlike him. My client had found a way of communicating with her husband through signs of snow and she had found an understanding of the way he now used his new language.

Smells

Many people notice smells as a form of receiving signs from their loved ones. Janice would smell her Nana's baking every time she was in a sticky situation, and she had the need from a cuddle from her Nana, who had passed some years earlier. Janice was convinced that it was her Nana because she only ever smelt the same baking when she truly felt the need for her Nana to be around, when she really missed her. The amazing thing about Janice was that she would smell her Nana's baking anywhere, including once while at the swimming baths.

One morning Janice had woken up upset and cried a lot. She closed her eyes and told her Nana how much she missed her, and she told her she was in need of a hug. Janice had been through hard few months and that week had been particularly hard. After her outburst, Janice decided to keep her mind occupied. She went to her local swimming baths looking forward to disconnecting from the world while she swam freely in the water. Amazingly while swimming at the swimming baths Janice actually smelt the smell of her Nana's baking. The smell was so strong that she asked another swimmer if they could also smell baking. Janice was quite shocked that the other swimmer couldn't smell baking. Janice knew instantly that it was a sign from her Nana.

Whenever Mark smelt the smell of his dad's perfume, he believed it was because his dad had come from the Other side to stand by him for a while. Mark only ever smelt his dad's perfume when he felt the need for his dad to be with him and he missed him the most. Mark couldn't work out how come at no other times did he ever smell his dad's perfume. Mark became a believer in the Afterlife due to this smell because Mark could find no other reasonable explanation for it.

When Marks daughter was married, everyone in the family missed Marks dad more so than ever. The family knew how much he loved his granddaughter. Mark told me that shortly after his daughter had become a married woman, he and his daughter danced their first wedding dance together. While proudly dancing with his daughter, Mark suddenly smelt the smell of his dad's perfume very strongly. He asked his daughter if she could smell it and he was relieved when she said she could smell her Granddads perfume clearly. Mark was amazed by the fact that not everyone in the room could smell the perfume.

Mark who was of a slightly scientific nature couldn't understand it and felt it was more than coincidence. He went around the event room with a notebook and pen and asked each one of the visitors if they could smell the strong perfume. He was astounded as he realised that only those who knew his dad could smell the smell, yet all the guests who didn't know his dad could not smell it at all. This to Mark was the proof he needed that his dad was still around.

I myself am pretty bad with smells, I can't tell one from another most of the time, but I do have a few smells that take me back to a memory or connect me to a certain person, not that I know the smell, but I know it's "that smell."

Music

I believe most of us have that special song that connects us to our loved one. I know hundreds of people who will hear a song play and believe it is a sign from their loved one who passed over. I am one of those people. I have certain songs that when I hear I know it's a sign. My dad's song, Right Here Waiting for You, is a song that every time I hear it I feel my dad is with me. Sometimes I am not too sure as to what he is actually trying to say to me when I hear his song play on the radio, but I do know he is with me at that time.

Many times, while giving a reading I have Spirit tell me about songs of importance to them. Sometimes I hear the song played in my mind and that can be slightly frustrating because if I'm not familiar with it I have to repeat it to my client in an almost singing tone, it's not pleasant to hear me sing.

However, other times I recognise the song and it is an important part of a message. It's a wonderful feeling to give a client the name of a song of importance between them and their loved one. I often wonder how I myself would feel if I went to a medium and they told me that my dad was singing me the song, Right Here Waiting for You. Although I have no doubt that my dad is with me it would be a touching and moving message for me that I would never forget.

I know people who also get messages from songs that are not necessary connected to their loved one and yet they take it as a sign as such. My best friend Beli had an experience some years ago where she would think of a close friend of hers who had passed and, in that instant, a song would play on her car radio, almost as if the song was a direct message from her friend. It was an incredible experience for her that lasted for some time, and even today in those times of need she will go for a drive and talk to her beloved friend and almost immediately a song of importance will come on the radio. These songs give her comfort in much needed times and I have no doubt that the Spirit of her friend is behind the radio stations choice of music.

Music is comforting to people on so many levels and is a sign I know many people use.

Numbers

Antonio swore he was receiving a sign. The number 33 had been following him around for a while. He was seeing it everywhere and in strange ways. The problem was Antonio didn't understand why he was seeing this number and it drove him crazy. He knew it was a sign, but he didn't know from who nor why. I never sat with Antonio to see if I could shed some light onto this and I haven't seen him for years, so I don't know if he ever found his reason. Antonio isn't the only person I know to have numbers follow them around. I know people who use numbers as signs. "I knew I was going to get the job because I saw even numbers all day," a client of mine named Ann told me. "How do you work that one out?" I asked with interest.

Ann told me that she and her best friend always played number games and when her friend died, she felt they continued to play. Ann told me she had received many signs since her friends passing and she understood them. Odd numbers were a no go, it was a sign from her friend to not do something or to look into something clearer. Even numbers, on the other hand, were a go ahead, a sign it's going to work out.

I am always surprised at how observant people are, I don't think I ever see random numbers around. However, if numbers were my sign, I'm sure I would see them and also feel the message with them. That's the magic of how individual and personal the sign language from Spirit is.

Names

Names are another sign often used by Spirits to communicate. Many people tend to pay attention to a person if they have the same name as a loved one who has passed. Recently I gave a reading for a woman named Maryanne who told me a story about how she believes her husband sent her a sign.

Maryanne and her husband Barry had been planning on selling the family home and moving into a bungalow. Before their home sold, they had to take it off the market due to Barry's illness. Sadly, Barry died, leaving Maryanne lost.

After talking to her daughter for some time. Maryanne felt she should return to the idea she had when Barry was alive and again, she put her house up for sale. Maryanne was quite scared about such a huge step without her dear husband Barry by her side helping with the sale, the packing, and the buying of a new home. Yet as scary as it was, Maryanne continued with her plan.

When Maryanne had the news of a viewing for her home, she had an overwhelming feeling of loneliness. After a lifetime with a loving husband, she was now taking large steps without him.

Maryanne told me that she instantly liked the woman who turned up at her home for a viewing. However, when she heard that the woman's surname was Thomson, Maryanne knew without doubt that Barry was helping her and that all would be ok. Thompson was the maiden name of Barry's mother.

It may seem like a small coincidence to some but for Maryanne, it made a huge difference. Maryanne was sure Barry was showing her that it would all work out and that he was with her. Maryanne did sell her house to the woman and bought a bungalow.

Many people across the globe use names as a way of communicating with Spirit.

Phyllis told me that she had entered the travel agents to cancel her holiday as she felt it was too soon after her mother's death. Although her family had encouraged Phyllis to continue with her holiday plan, she felt somewhat bad going on holiday so soon after the passing of her dearly loved mother. When Phyllis walked into the travel agent, she sat in front of a young girl and explained to her that she intended to cancel her holiday. The young travel agent brought her chair closer to Phyllis and looked intensely at her. "Are you sure this is what you want?" the agent asked Phyllis. At that point, Phyllis noticed the girl's name tag. Her name was May, the same name as Phyllis's mother.

Phyllis felt it was a sign from her mother and immediately changed her mind and continued with her holiday plans.

I met Phyllis while she was on that holiday, she was having a great time and was pleased she hadn't cancelled the holiday. Now Phyllis is alert and looks out for signs from her Spirit loved ones, usually finding them in names.

Electrical Goods

Spirit has other ways of communicating with us that are not regular signs yet are taken as a sign at that moment. Where you can take a message from an event, yet it may be random and never happen again, or it may happen a few times but it's not that one thing you connect to when you think of a sign from your loved one. Like when Spirit use electrical goods to send us messages that they are with us.

It's a bit like having a hello from the Other side. I remember when my aunty Pam died, on the day of her funeral I was sitting in the living room at my Nana's house watching the TV with my children when suddenly the TV switched off. I got up and turned it on again and five minutes later, again it went off. I could have thought it was a fault in the TV and left it as so, however, I felt in that moment that it was my aunt telling me she was ok on the Other side. It was a hello from her. I had travelled a long way to see her at the chapel of rest and yet I knew I wouldn't be able to go to the funeral as I had my children with me, they were young and in prams. Therefore, I felt Pam had come to see me that day.

Electrical goods that unexpectedly switch on or off, lights flickering. Computers doing random things on its own, TV turning off or over, are just a few of the many electrical phenomenon I have heard of over the years. Of course, electrical faults could be to blame. My Nana's TV could have been getting prepared to break down. Nevertheless, a sign is about what we feel when we receive it. The TV could blow up in front of me and I may not think anything of it on a spiritual level. Yet the moment the TV went off on the day of my aunt's funeral I just knew inside it was a sign. I feel this is the way most people see signs, they feel them.

Signs come in all shapes and forms and there is no true translation book to become fluent in understanding the sign language. It's also an evolving language. Years ago, I never thought a feather was a sign, today it's an important part of my guidance. I have somehow incorporated it. Not only am I picking up new signs I am also asking for direct signs. Sometimes I will say ok show me a

215

daffodil if I am on the right track and voila, I get a daffodil sent to me in some form.

My Own Signs

While writing this book I was bombarded by very clear direct signs from Spirit to continue, even when I criticized my writing, my editing, and my style. Those down days where I wondered about who cares about what I have to say. Convinced people preferred to read about doctors who had near death experiences or stories that included an encounter with Jesus, or at the least, from a medium who is a celebrity. Yet I was encouraged to write, and this book almost flowed from my fingertips. However, being me, I needed to make it clear. I was opening myself up for ridicule with this book and I, at least, wanted to be clear on the signs that were the reason for me continuing.

Although the signs were clear and direct, like my chapter title repeated to me by people on the same day of writing, mere coincidence, no I do not believe in coincidence, I never have done.

To get even clearer I started to ask Spirit for signs. "If you are happy with that chapter, show me a blossom tree."

My friend returned from holiday that same day and showed me her holiday pictures, almost every picture was of blossom trees.

I began to ask for more specific signs, I became needier. I asked for stranger, harder signs. One day I asked Spirit that if they liked my chapter name then to send me a rainbow butterfly. I looked out all day for the appearance of a coloured butterfly. I was in awe in the evening when I logged onto Facebook to find some random person had sent me photos of rainbow butterflies.

The signs continued to appear to me throughout the writing of this book. Although I no longer asked for signs as I felt it was needless by now. It was obvious I was going ahead with the book and now I no longer needed confirmation that it would be ok. I had overcome my barrier thanks to the signs, and I was writing from the heart. The last sign I had asked for was blue grass, I must have been in a rush when I asked for blue grass and I rather regretted it afterwards as I realised this might never happen. It did not actually exist therefore it was unlikely I would see it.

Three days later, I was emptying my junk mail on my email. I briefly looked at the title of the emails as in between the Nigerian king who is going to leave me his millions and my non-existent PayPal account needing all my details again, sometimes I get interesting stuff put out with the trash. In big letters, I saw the title Blue Grass. Without praying long enough for it not to be a virus I clicked onto it and was amazed to see a strange picture of a field and in the background was clearly blue grass. When we order a specific sign then it doesn't get lost in translation. We know what we want and why we want it, and Spirit are willing to help us always.

I feel that apart from common signs like feathers and personal signs, like Lucy and her safety pin from her grandmother. I do feel we can actually be specific and ask for a sign. As Janet did when I suggested she ask for a feather from her son Robert or like I did with my blue grass.

Spirit sends us signs constantly; they want us to learn their new sign language so they can communicate and guide us and most importantly that we know they still exist in the Spirit world. That the Spirit world is real, it does exist, and it is a place, and they are living there.

I know that when I return home to the Spirit world, I will spend as much energy as I need to send signs to my children and family, so they know I am with them. I will use any reference and any chance I can to send signs to my children, to protect them and guide them. I feel I am no different from most people and I understand why Spirit signs are important to both the living and those who have passed.

CHAPTER 15

We'll Meet Again

The news of my Nana's death was shocking to me, at first, I could not believe that the woman I loved and who had loved me in return unconditional since I was born had left my world. Although she was living in the UK and me in Spain, she had been like the screensaver of my life, always there in the background.

I clearly remembered her last visit to see my mum and me in Spain, just a year previous. On meeting her at the airport with my uncle Donald who had travelled with her, I realized her mind had deteriorated somewhat. As we sat on the coach from Alicante airport to Benidorm I sat next to her, I couldn't stop holding her and hugging her. "Do you remember me?" I asked her with hope. "Yes, I do," she replied to me, almost whispering. "I'm your favourite granddaughter," I told her, just to make sure.

"Bugger off," she said to me as she smiled. I knew then that she knew exactly who I was and if she didn't, I knew who she was.

Those following weeks she stayed with us were interesting, at first, she could not remember my children or Andres but within a week she remembered them clearly, she remembered all details of years gone by, like when I got married and memories of when Nicole and Danny were small. Her memory was usually good. One evening she sat and told me how she and my Granddad had met, the name of the street and every detail.

I spent as much time as I could with her while she was on holiday, popping up for a cup of tea with her between readings and spending as much none work time with her as possible. Often, I would curl up with her on the couch, as I had done as a child. She was as loving and gentle as she always had been with me.

I cried like a baby at the airport when I said goodbye to her. "I won't ever see her again," I cried as my mum hugged me and reassured me.

You can imagine my excitement when the following year Donald phoned my mum to inform us, he and my Nana were booking another holiday. I smiled to myself as I thought about how soon I would be hugging her again.

I was writing this book at the time, and I had just finished the chapter Fields of Gold, when I realized I was shattered and I went to bed. That night I had a weird dream, in the dream, I was desperately looking for a sign from Spirit. The entire dream was about me looking for a sign, except for the ending of the dream where I was clearly shown I had to be strong. I woke up feeling stronger than ever. I was just about to leave for work when the phone rang, my mum was crying down the phone. My Nana was dead.

My uncle Donald had said goodnight to her as he did every night and the next morning, he found her dead in bed. It was devastating for Donald and his wife Maxine and their three girls because my Nana had stayed with them for years and was a large part of their daily life.

I was in cold shock, I went through the motions of getting a flight back to the UK with my mum, but somewhere at the back of my mind, I didn't really believe she was dead. I knew this day would come, she was 89 years of age, it was clear she would die at some point. However, I didn't expect it then.

In a way, I was looking forward to going to the chapel of rest so I could see for myself she had really gone, almost as if I had to see it to believe it. I needed my moment with her in a dramatic way so I could say goodbye.

When I reach the UK, I was told due to an infection they had to close my Nana's coffin. I was grateful the funeral directors had closed the coffin and didn't allow me to see her if she looked in a bad way, yet still I needed my moment of drama.

I decided to go and sit with her anyway, even with a closed coffin I needed to say goodbye to the woman I loved so much.

As I walked into the room, I felt strong, I walked closer, and I saw her name engraved on a gold plaque upon the coffin. My Nana's name was shining at me, and I knew this was as real as it gets. She was really dead.

I sobbed as I thanked her for loving me for so many years, then I touched her coffin and said, "I hope you enjoy your fields of gold Nana." I then kissed her name plaque, leaving a big lipstick mark over her name. Unsure whether to wipe the lipstick off or not I decided to keep it on, let her go with my kisses, I thought to myself.

If the reality of her death hit me at the funeral home, it was the reality of her last years of her life that hit me as I entered my uncle Donald and my aunty Maxine's home. The house smelt strongly of my Nana, the conservatory was set up so she had the most comfortable chair, a television, a telephone next to the doors of the patio, for those days she wanted fresh air but didn't want to sit in the garden. Entering her bedroom was hard, it was almost like walking into her life.

She had a beautiful bedroom with a large window and a double bed, she was surrounded by all her treasures and had an attached bathroom stacked full of all her creams and perfumes. Her wardrobe was bulging with bits and pieces she loved to buy. She had a wonderful life staying at Donald and Maxine's. Donald had given up his day job some while back to take on night work so he could take her shopping, one of her biggest hobbies, or he would take her on day trips. She was out and about every day. She had been catered for in every way possible, treated with tenderness and love with all her needs met and she wanted for nothing. I realized how lucky she had been.

As I looked around her life, I knew she had lived a long and happy life, although she had a lifetime habit of moaning, it was clear she was happy, Even the day before she died Donald had taken her to a huge market where she loved to go and shop. She was always shopping.

In her bedroom above her bed, was almost like a photo album of her life, pictures of the many family members that had been taken over the years. Next to a picture of herself was a picture of me. I took great comfort in that picture.

I felt at peace with my Nana's death when I left her bedroom. Somehow, I knew it had been her time to go.

I was, however, not happy that she had died, and I had not received any sign or pre-warning. I worked full time as a psychic medium, surely, I should have known my dear Nana was going to die.

I complained to anyone who would listen for a while "I had no sign," I said almost blaming the listener.

Then I sat and thought about it in more detail, did I really have no sign? No, I didn't in the sense that I didn't know my Nana was going to die on that day. However, if I looked at it after the event, I knew the year before that I would not see her again, as I waved goodbye at the airport sobbing into my mother's arms, I knew then it would be the last time I saw her.

A few days before my Nana had died, I gave a reading for a 65-year-old woman, her mother had died some time previously, and she was still grief-stricken. "Even though she was old, it still hurts to lose them," the woman told me through tears.

"I know," I replied. "Obviously not like losing a younger member of the family, but it's still a loss that has a profound effect, after all, she had been in your life forever," I said to her.

The woman stopped crying and said to me, "you're the first one who has understood what I'm trying to say, everyone keeps telling me to get over it because she was old, so she was expected to die."

At this point I was thinking about my Nana, she's been there all my life also.

I couldn't quite get my Nana out of my mind that evening and I called her on the phone, but no one was in. I was going to call back the next day but regretfully I was busy and unable to do.

The next day as I entered my apartment, I found a white feather outside the lift. I thought it strange how it was placed directly in front of the lift, almost as if it was in the centre of my way. I picked up the feather and wondered how a feather had entered my hallway thirteen flights up with no open window. I popped my feather in my purse and entered my apartment. As often happens in my life, the moment I enter my home I am informed of things we need to buy at the shop. Without taking my shoes off, I went back out and to the local store.

On returning, as the lift doors opened, I found another white feather in the exact same place. I stood mesmerized for a moment, I picked it up and realized it was a sign, yet I didn't know what it meant? This great psychic didn't understand the message that was being shown.

That night I worked hard on this book, somehow the folder of my first book, Always by Your Side, opened, I hadn't touched anything so I wasn't sure why it had opened on its own.

I quickly scrolled down the screen as I noticed something odd, every word, NANA in my book was highlighted and where my word program says, find a word, the word NANA had been typed in, hence it had been highlighted.

Although looking back I could say that was a pretty big hint, it did not say to me, or, at least, I did not take it to mean that my Nana was going to die.

My book then jumped to the last page and my last words, Till We Meet Again, was staring at me from the screen. I wondered what it meant. I couldn't work it out, so I turned my computer off and decided to listen to music. Somehow, I found myself listening to the song, We'll Meet Again, by Vera Lyne, it reminded me of my dear friend Dee and the times we would often sing this song when were in our small spiritual group, the most inspiring days of my life.

That next day I had a reading for a niece of the woman who owned the shop where I work. I had already given her a reading some months previous, and her father had given her many messages, one of them had been about feathers. Laura connected so well with the message regarding the feathers and what followed was a huge feather connection for her. Laura then had a feather tattooed on her back. When I saw the photo of the tattoo, I fell in love with it.

When Laura arrived for her reading, I had heard of my Nana's death just hours before and in a way, I thought I shouldn't be working but because it hadn't really hit me yet, I felt that working with Spirit was the best place for me, after all, my Nana was with Spirit now, so I wanted to be as close to her as I could be.

Laura received several messages that day and one of the messages was to watch out for the yellow flowers, in my mind, I saw two yellow roses, but I didn't take them literate. Instead, I told Laura to watch out for the yellow flowers, they were her next sign. We laughed as she told me she could see herself coming for her next reading with another tattoo of yellow flowers on her back.

For some reason, I felt a connection with that message and after she left, I thought I would take her message for myself. I decided I also wanted a sign of yellow flowers to tell me my Nana was still with me, a bit of comfort for my own grieving soul. Even though I knew my Nana would now be happy in the Spirit world, I knew how it worked. I was still human, and it still hurt like hell. So, I asked for a sign of two yellow roses.

When I arrived back in the UK for her funeral, I went to my uncle Marks house and the first thing I noticed was the beautiful yellow rose tree in his garden. I smiled as I thought, yes, she is with me. Although it was nice to see the rose tree, it didn't quite give me the comfort I had hoped for.

Later on, that evening, my uncle Donald showed me the program he had planned for the funeral. A lovely card with everything that was to be said during the service. On the front of the card was a picture of my Nana. Tears fell like memories down my cheek as I looked at her picture. I placed the booklet in my bag and for the next few days, I carried it around with me. It became handy when family members who were traveling for the funeral asked me where the funeral was to be held and what time. I was often pulling out the booklet to repeat the time and address to my cousins.

On the day of the funeral, I felt rather sorry for myself, it had been important for me to see two yellow roses and so far, other than a yellow rose tree I hadn't had my sign. For once, I wasn't a medium, instead I was a granddaughter who desperately missed her Nana.

On the day of the funeral, several family members and I were just about to leave my uncle Donald's house when he gave us the booklet of the funeral.

"I already have mine," I said to him as I was about to return the one he had just handed me. Abruptly I pulled it back, there on the front page was the picture of my Nana, and underneath was an image of two yellow roses.

I couldn't believe I had been carrying the booklet around for days and pulling it out to look at it and yet I had missed the image underneath that Donald had chosen. I had received my sign days before, but I had missed it.

Donald had also chosen my Nana's favourite song to be played as we left the church.

"We'll meet again."

CHAPTER 16

Heaven Can Wait

It had been quite some while since I had entered the Spirit world. The older I became the less and less I seemed to enter, certainly not as regular as I did when I was younger.

This one day I was lying on my bed, the TV was on quietly in the background and I was relaxing as I watched the sea from my bedroom window. The waves were loud, and I closed my eyes and listened. Unexpectedly, I could no longer hear the waves and I found myself in the Spirit world. I recognised the path ahead of me with excitement. It had been a long time since I had last walked along this pathway. I wondered if I had fallen asleep on my bed and yet I felt I hadn't, I had just closed my eyes and found myself on the pathway. I smiled as I walked past the colourful flowers along the way, towards the hill.

At the foot of the old familiar hill, I felt an adrenalin rush and I couldn't wait to get to the tree. As I excitedly headed for my old hang out place under the large tree, I felt somewhat disappointed as I looked around and realised that neither George nor any of my old friends were there.

I looked around me, the beauty of the Afterlife spreading for miles and miles. I felt truly grateful as I heard the sound of nature within the silence. I looked at the old tree, remembering the many times I had played beneath it, how I had grown from a baby to a child, to a woman under that same tree.

I remembered all the friends I had met over the years. All the conversations and all the knowledge this one spot of Heaven had brought me.

I was deep in thought remembering a lifetime of visits when I noticed a movement from behind the tree.

I headed closer towards the tree to see what the movement was and as I got closer, from behind the tree appeared my Nana.

She smiled at me, and I ran over to her, although I am a grown woman, I ran to her as any six-year-old girl would run into their Nana's arms.

She hugged me and I cried as I told her I loved her. "I know, I know," she said softly as she held me tight.

I immediately asked her if she was happy, I knew it was a silly question, but it almost seemed automatic. "I'm very happy," she told me.

She was wearing a light pink flowered dress and although she didn't quite look like she had when she had died, yet she looked the same as she always looked. It was like looking at a friend who I hadn't seen for years, only instead of looking older she looked somewhat younger. Yet, without doubt, she looked like I always remembered her.

She sat down under the tree, and I sat next to her. We talked for what seemed like hours, we talked about everyone she had met since she had passed. She told me she was with her daughter, my aunty Pam and with her son, David. She spoke to me about other people she had met up with since her passing, a few of them were old neighbours whose names I had forgotten.

We spoke about my uncle Donald. It had been hard for him since she left. She told me she would always be with him; she would always be by his side. I placed my head on her shoulder, I didn't want this moment to end. I wanted to stay with her forever.

Slowly my Nana stood up, she wiped her dress down and told me it was time for me to go.

"I don't want to go," I said to her stubbornly, reminding myself of the little girl who had refused to leave from the very same spot on the hill some 30 years previous.

"You have to go, your mum, your children, your husband, they all need you," she said to me gently. In that instant, I remembered my family and I knew it was true. I had to leave and return to home. I just wanted a little bit longer.

"And you have to finish your book," she said to me as she bent down and picked up a small wicker basket. I hadn't noticed the basket until then.

"I have finished my book," I said to her, rather pleased that she knew I had written my second book.

"No darling, you have one more chapter to finish," she whispered to me.

Puzzled I asked her, "what chapter?"

"This one," she replied.

I smiled at her as I stood up beside her.

"Come on, bugger off, you have to go," she said to me.

I reached out for her, and I hugged her. I have met many Spirits on the hill, I have spent a lifetime playing and dancing and telling stories. I have met friends like George and other Spirits, yet I never expected to see my Nana standing in my play land.

"What are you going to do?" I asked her.

She laughed at me, "I'm going to bake," she continued "I bet all these years you have been coming here, you never realised that this tree is an apple tree, did you?"

My Nana reached up and picked a large apple off the tree.

Then she placed the apple in the basket and smiled at me.

"No Nana, I never realised it was an apple tree," I replied to her quite amazed at the realization that throughout all these years I had never once wondered what kind of tree it was.

"Go Gaynor, it's not your time, not yet."

I opened my eyes and found myself lying on my bed listening to the waves. I was back in my earthly life.

I slowly got off my bed. I couldn't believe the experience I had just had, and that's something considering all the experiences I have lived through over the years. I felt happy as I walked over to my bedroom window remembering every detail of what had just happened to me.

As I looked out across the sparkling Mediterranean Sea, I noticed children playing and swimming. They were enjoying this world as much as I had spent a lifetime enjoying the next. As I watched the children and heard their laughter, I thought about my own children.

Nicole had almost slipped through my fingers, a young loving woman now, who was happily finding her own world. I loved her so much and I was so proud of the woman she had become. She had her own life now that included more than her family. She had found a man who loved her. I felt my heart jump with joy as I saw her shine from within with love.

I thought of Danny, he was almost a man now, so soft and gentle. He was a caring soul who was happy to be around the home still. In a selfish way, I was glad he hadn't flown the nest yet, although I knew that his day would come and again my heart would burst with joy when his time comes to find love.

I thought about my life, two wonderful children, a loving

husband. A mother who is my best friend.

I work as a medium, a job I love and have spent a lifetime working to improve. I have a good relationship with people I work with. I go out with my family and my mother, for meals, for a drink, even going for a cup of coffee can bring buckets of laughter. I love sharing my knowledge of the place of the Afterlife. I love giving messages from Spirits to my clients. I often remember the lesson I learnt from the Spirit of Albert, treasure the small things, as they are what really matters.

I love the Spirit world and I have had some amazing times while there, but I love my life more. If I had never entered Heaven, I would have never known what amazing beauty waited for me, and I am truly grateful for being able to live life in the two worlds.

However, as I realised that my Nana had 89 years of children, grandchildren, and great-grandchildren. As I remembered, it was her who made my flowers at my wedding, I knew that is what life is all about. Memories, each moment is a memory, each memory is the reason I am here.

It's the memories of life that are precious, the love that we feel and the laughter that we are able to share.

I left my bedroom and walked around my apartment. I had no luxuries inside my small, rented sea front apartment, and yet the sea view was a gift from God. However, it was the memories I had created in my home that made it special for me. We had shared the love as a family.

I popped my head into Nicole's bedroom, it was a maze of

clothes and shoes. I smiled as I saw her new high heels, they must have been at least two storeys high. A pang of nostalgia came over me as I realised, she was hardly there now she was busy with her own life. I wondered what her future would be like. I couldn't wait to be a grandmother and I knew she would be a wonderful mum. I wondered who she would marry. She was still young, and she had plenty of time for babies and marriage.

Still, I became excited as I thought about the wonderful adventure we had ahead of us. I smiled as I realised that it would be my mum making her flowers on her wedding day, just as my Nana did on mine. I could imagine my mum making a fuss and creating a perfect bouquet of flowers, probably the cake and the buffet would also be on her to do list.

I wondered at what point my mum had become my best friend. I wasn't sure exactly when it happened, I was just happy that she was. I loved her so much and I knew without doubt that I was the love of her life.

I gently closed Nicole's bedroom door, I felt so blessed to have her in my life.

To dramatize my nostalgia slightly, I decided to open my son's bedroom door. He smiled at me as I walked in and sat on his bed. He was heavily into a game on his computer, I sat and watched him, and I realised he was in his own world, much as I had just been in my own world, only different by the places and the realities of both.

I wondered what kind of life he would have, I assumed he would work in computers because that was what he had always loved to do.

However, he also liked to cook and although I couldn't see him working in a kitchen, I imagined him making wonderful meals for his future wife. I could see him inviting me and the family to his home on Sundays for a nice meal.

I became excited as I wondered what career he would have, what his wife would be like, how many children he would bring into the world.

I could not imagine anyone loving him more than I did. However, I got excited as I thought about the magical memories that had not yet been created. I didn't want to know the future of the life of my children, instead, I wanted to live it.

In that instant I realised that I have a lot more memories I needed to create and to enjoy. I could almost hear the echoes of the laughter we had yet to come as a family.

I know when I pass over into Spirit, I will enjoy to the fullest my life in the Afterlife. I know I will have a happy time in Heaven when there. I will play in the fields I have played in so often since I was a child. I will swim in the lakes and oceans I have swum in over the years when visiting. I will explore the Afterlife just as I have always done, with joy, wonder, and follow each road until the next.

Although I know without doubt, that Heaven is a real place. Although I know that one day it will be my home, yet I know that this world is my home just now and that in all honestly, Heaven can wait.

ABOUT THE AUTHOR

I am currently working in Benidorm and run an online spiritual school where I give courses, workshops, and masterclasses. I Also offer coaching. My website is www.gaynorcarrillo.com

Feel free to contact me at gaynorcarrillo@hotmail.com

Thank you so much for taking the time to read my words. I am now working on my next book. If you enjoyed this read and you are able, please leave a review on Amazon it would mean a lot to me.

Until the next one, thank you. Gaynor

Made in the USA
Las Vegas, NV
06 April 2024

88343549R00152